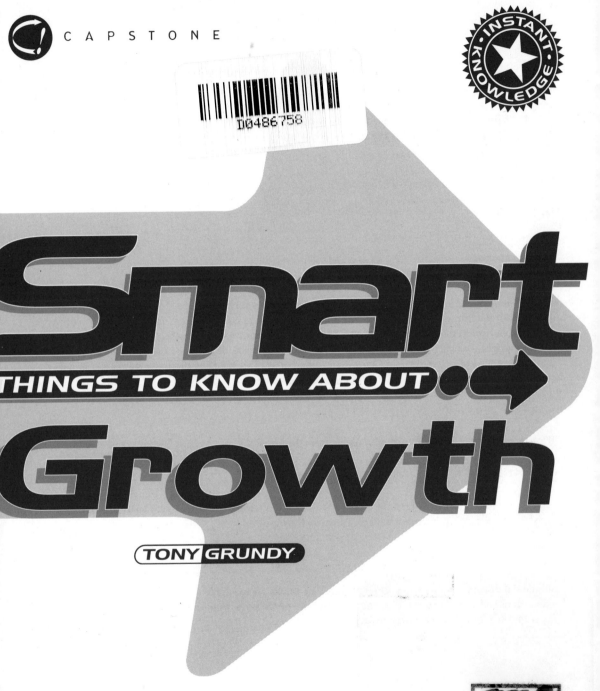

# Smart

## THINGS TO KNOW ABOUT

# Growth

**TONY GRUNDY**

First Published 2003 by
Capstone Publishing Limited (a Wiley company)
8 Newtec Place
Magdalen Road
Oxford
OX4 1RE
United Kingdom
http://www.capstoneideas.com

CIP catalogue records for this book are available from the British Library and the US Library of Congress

ISBN 1-84112-052-9

Typeset in 11/15pt Sabon by Sparks Computer Solutions Ltd, Oxford, UK (http://www.sparks.co.uk)
Printed and bound by T.J. International Ltd, Padstow, Cornwall

# Contents

*What is Smart?*                                                    vii

1   Introduction                                                      1

2   Managing Growth Drivers and Competitive Pressure                37

3   Diagnosis of Growth Issues                                       75

4   Cunning Options for Growth                                       95

5   Managing Organic Growth – With Success                          145

6   Managing Acquisitive Growth – With Success                      169

7   Implementing Growth Strategies                                  211

8  Valuing Growth Strategies                    237

9  Growth Checklists                            263

10  Conclusion                                   285

*Index*                                           297

# What is Smart?

The *Smart* series is a new way of learning. *Smart* books will improve your understanding and performance in some of the critical areas you face today like *customers*, *strategy*, *change*, *e-commerce*, *brands*, *influencing skills*, *knowledge management*, *finance*, *teamworking*, and *partnerships*.

*Smart* books summarize accumulated wisdom as well as providing original cutting-edge ideas and tools that will take you out of theory and into action.

The widely respected business guru Chris Argyris points out that even the most intelligent individuals can become ineffective in organizations. Why? Because we are so busy working that we fail to learn about ourselves. We stop reflecting on the changes around us. We get sucked into the patterns of behaviour that have produced success for us in the past, not realizing that it may no longer be appropriate for us in the fast-approaching future.

There are three ways the *Smart* series helps prevent this happening to you:

- by increasing your self awareness;

- by developing your understanding, attitude and behaviour; and

- by giving you the tools to challenge the status quo that exists in your organization.

Smart people need smart organizations. You could spend a third of your career hopping around in search of the Holy Grail, or you could begin to create your own smart organization around you today.

Finally, a reminder that books don't change the world, people do. And although the *Smart* series offers you the brightest wisdom from the best practitioners and thinkers, these books throw the responsibility on you to *apply* what you're learning to your work.

Because the truly smart person knows that reading a book is the start of the process and not the end ...

As Eric Hoffer says, 'In times of change, learners inherit the world, while the learned remain beautifully equipped to deal with a world that no longer exists.'

*David Firth*
*Smartmaster*

# 1

# Introduction

## *Why grow?*

Whilst growth is frequently a central objective for most organizations, its actual value is often imprecisely understood. For growth is not a good-in-itself thing, but is merely a vehicle for achieving other important goals. Those goals may include:

- profitability;

- increasing shareholder value;

- building market dominance;

- developing capability;

- protecting and strengthening the business;

- creating future opportunities;

- future positioning;

- creating exciting career paths; and

- providing an ongoing sense of challenge.

Unless you do have clear growth goals and also a growth strategy, then the business can easily slide into a sense of complacency and begin to go backwards. To grow requires the drive to reinvent yourself – as in our Madonna example below – to rethink 'what business you are in', and perhaps also to attempt to change the mindset of the industry itself.

*An unlikely strategy case – the Madonna phenomenon: from geisha girl to cowgirl*

The 1980s belong to Madonna – the star who delighted to shock with her songs, her dress, her videos. Without possessing the greatest voice in the universe, Madonna's drive, personality and persistence made her a true superstar.

But whilst history is littered with examples of how superstars have faded – either gradually or sometimes into oblivion – Madonna's ability to reinvent herself has just grown and grown. By the late 1990s and early 2000s, Madonna was still in the process of metamorphosis, with best-selling CDs like *Ray of Light* and *Music*. Her videos show her progressing from geisha girl through to cowgirl. And her net worth is still increasing …

This book makes the assumption that you are very interested in growing your business. It also assumes that you may currently lack clarity about relative priorities of your growth objectives, your growth strategy, and also how you will implement it, and that you want to use its ideas to shift gear into a different, higher quality, growth path.

## Short exercise – understanding your growth objectives

Now, in Table 1.1 below, rate your growth objectives as a management team on a scale of importance of 1–5.

Table 1.1   Understanding your growth objectives.

| Growth goal | Extremely important 5 | Very important 4 | Moderately important 3 | Low importance 2 | Very low importance 1 |
|---|---|---|---|---|---|
| Profitability (short-term) | | | | | |
| Profitability (long-term) | | | | | |
| Market dominance | | | | | |
| Capability for development | | | | | |
| Protecting/ strengthening | | | | | |
| Future opportunities | | | | | |
| Future positioning | | | | | |
| Better career paths | | | | | |
| Sense of challenge | | | | | |

Points to consider in the above include the following.

- What is your rationale for the trade-off between short- and longer-term profitability?

- What is the balance between more aggressive and offensive growth strategy and protecting the business?

- Have you given sufficient importance to 'softer' growth goals, like capability development, better career paths, a sense of challenge?

To achieve sustainable growth requires a clearly defined growth strategy. To put this into perspective we will need to say a little about the role of strategic planning and of strategic thinking in particular.

Too often, strategic planning is implemented with a principal focus on a company's internal position, and with the more obvious and immediate opportunities which spring to mind. Strategic plans are often dominated by lists of strategies which are in effect goals – the 'what' rather than the 'how'. Company planning documents are equally dominated by more quantitative results of assumed strategies, rather than with innovative, strategic thinking.

This book aims to correct this imbalance by showing how strategic thinking – if pursued in a focused and step-by-step fashion – can produce sustainable, value-led growth. But, as we begin, there is still some ambiguity around the very notion of 'strategy'. So what *is* strategy?

A traditional definition of strategy is that it is the 'how' of moving from your current position to where you need/want to be in the future, with sustainable competitive advantage. This definition usefully spells out four major elements:

- we need to know our current position;

- we need to imagine our future position;

- we need to have the 'how' of getting there; and

- this 'how' needs to create a sustainable competitive advantage.

In the rest of this chapter, we look at:

- growth at Tesco – an example of successful growth;

- gap analysis;

- growth strategy and the 'cunning plan';

- the growth cycle;

- growth and the strategy mix;

- routes to growth;

- the growth process and techniques; and

- an overview of the book.

## Growth at Tesco

In 1990 Tesco was very much placed as the number two UK supermarket chain. Sainsbury's was well established as the market leader, with 'Good Food Costs Less at Sainsbury's' as its strapline. Asda, which expanded rapidly in the late 1980s, had become over-geared (with high borrowings) and less profitable.

Tesco's then chairman, McLauren, launched the company in an aggressive direction of not merely catching up with Sainsbury's, but of overtaking them too. By adopting an aggressive expansion – through larger, up-to-date superstores, with better products, aimed at the total family shop – Tesco sought to leapfrog Sainsbury's.

The Tesco stores were stylized as the Essex barn. Whilst being expensive to build, this image helped Tesco to position itself as offering comparable quality to that of Sainsbury's. Its product range was considerably improved, enabling it to move away from the philosophy of 'pile it high and sell it cheap', which had been its successful growth strategy in the late 1960s and 70s.

In the early to mid-1990s, Tesco mounted a very aggressive challenge to Sainsbury's. This took the form of a number of important and offensive growth strategies, which included the following.

- Tesco Clubcard – Tesco's pioneering loyalty card helped acquire an estimated 1% extra market share.

- New formats – Tesco experimented with Tesco Metro (small city centre stores which attacked Marks & Spencer foods), Tesco Extra (updated and expanded out-of-town large stores), and Tesco Express (the drive-in petrol store).

- Product diversification – major successes were gained in the diversification into non-foods (including clothing, household goods and appliances).

A major supplier on Tesco's senior managers: 'Tesco's, oh you know that senior manager? You ask me what the difference is between Tesco and Sainsbury's over the period of the 1990s. Well, that particular manager would not conceivably have held the equivalent job at another supermarket chain, which I won't name … no, he probably wouldn't have been allowed to work for the company …'

- Financial services – in the late 1990s Tesco entered the financial services market, with savings accounts and basic insurance-related products.

- Homeshopping – in 1996 Tesco began to develop its Homeshopping strategy (later known as Tesco Direct and as Tesco.com).

- International expansion – by 2001, Tesco planned (within a medium-term time frame) to have nearly half of its square footage located outside the UK.

These combined-growth breakthroughs effectively doubled Tesco's market share between 1990 and 2000. But what was the underlying basis of Tesco's success? Tesco, Sainsbury's, Asda and Safeway have similar access to the key resources for growth – sites, finance, products, process and systems. Probably the big difference is to be found in Tesco's people-base and its mindset, as illustrated by the next examples.

*Smart quotes*

'For me, it is remarkable that in five years Tesco has moved from being a UK-based supermarket chain to become an international mixed retail and services business. This rapid transformation is based on clarity at the top and a tremendous creativity and energy in making it happen quickly.'

Paul Mancey, Tesco

'This obsession with our customers, their needs, and how these must be changing, means that you should not expect us to go on opening large edge-of-town superstores long after the need for new ones has passed. Expect … continual evolution: expect us to provide a mix of formats in different locations … to meet special needs of customers in each location.'

Terry Leahey, CEO of Tesco (Tesco's Annual Report, 2000)

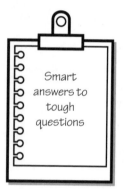

Smart
answers to
tough
questions

Q: Why was Tesco so successful in its growth strategy over the last ten years?

A: Tesco has:

- focused on a small number of breakthroughs (at particular times);
- been determined in its will to win;
- followed the processes examined in this book (especially those in Chapters 4 and 7); and
- aggressively developed the strategic thinking of its key managers.

## Gap analysis

Gap analysis is one of the least well-used tools of analysis of growth strategies. Even now, in this new millennium, it is still quite rare to see it in formal use. This is despite its once-upon-a-time popularity, both for corporate planning and for marketing strategy.

An example of gap analysis for a maturing company is illustrated in Fig. 1.1. Here we see the core business activities facing competitive pressure and a fall in expected growth rate, squeezing operating profit. Although future international development and new business activities fulfil part of corporate aspirations, there still remains a significant gap.

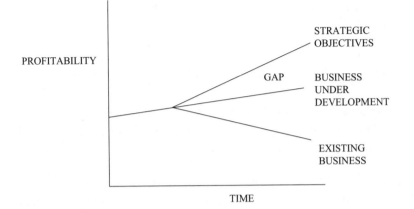

**Fig. 1.1** Strategic gap analysis.

The key benefits of gap analysis are that it:

- provides a very clear focus for sketching your aspirations for the business;

- links in with the strategic breakthroughs required in order to move the business forward; and

- emphasizes the longer and medium term and is not just confined to the shorter term.

The potential drawbacks of gap analysis are that it:

- is frequently used on its own – without supporting techniques; and

- typically results in superficial thinking, rather than truly creative analysis of potential breakthroughs.

What better a company to illustrate gap analysis with than Amazon.com in the early 2000s.

## Amazon.com – managing the gap: a brief analysis

Amazon.com was founded in 1995 to exploit the Internet for order-taking and fulfilment of those orders, in relation to books. This was later extended to CDs and videos, which had very similar buying-cycle characteristics.

Amazon scored with customers, through being cheaper and by being more convenient for some (as you do not have to go to a bookstore), and also because it offered a vast range of titles. Not only did this expand the breadth of choice, but it also meant that orders could be delivered much quicker than through the traditional high street outlets, where orders for out-of-stock books could typically take two to four weeks to fulfil. Amazon's website also sought to be value-added, by guiding readers towards a choice of title.

Amazon's initial vision was therefore to become the world's leading 'virtual' supplier of books, accomplishing this through cost-leadership underpinned by Internet technology. Amazon's figures (in $million) for the four full years of operation to 1998 are reproduced in Table 1.2 below.

Two things are immediately evident from this analysis. First, that Amazon was growing at an incredible rate (and in fact, by 2000, a quarter's sales were approximately the same as 1998's total sales). Second, its losses were enormous.

Whilst one does not necessarily expect to immediately make a profit (let alone one sufficient to cover the cost of capital) in a start-up, launch, or even the development phase of growth, the question must arise: when will

**Table 1.2**  Amazon figures.

| | 1995 | 1996 | 1997 | 1998 | As a percentage of sales |
|---|---|---|---|---|---|
| Sales | 0.5 | 16 | 148 | 610 | — |
| Cost of sales | 0.4 | 12 | 119 | 475 | — |
| Gross profit | 0.1 | 4 | 29 | 135 | 22.1 |
| **Operating expenses:** | | | | | |
| Marketing and sales | 0.2 | 6 | 40 | 133 | 21.8 |
| Product development | 0.1 | 2 | 14 | 47 | 7.7 |
| Administration | 0.1 | 2 | 7 | 15 | 2.4 |
| Acquisition write-downs | — | — | — | 50 | 8.2 |
| Total | 0.4 | 10 | 61 | 245 | 40.1 |
| Loss from operations | (0.3) | (6) | (32) | (110) | 18 |
| Net interest cost | — | — | 1 | (12) | 1.9 |
| **Net profit (loss)** | (3) | (6) | 31 | (122) | 19.9 |

Amazon begin to generate profit and cash sufficient to cover its shareholders' aspirations?

Even stripping out the 8.2% of sales written off as acquisition costs, Amazon would still be losing 12.1% of its total sales on average. And if we were able to apply the thinking discussed later on in this book (particularly that in Chapter 3 concerning the diagnosis of growth issues), we would see the following factors.

- Whilst external growth drivers are highly positive, Internet-buying of books may not necessarily become the market's primary method of delivery.

- The competitive forces for this market – given the cosy existence of substitute channels and the higher propensity for customers to shop around – severely limit margin potential.

- Amazon's aggressive discounting strategy leaves it with little room to widen its margins.

- Whilst Amazon is a thrusting, technology-led and innovative company, will it have the necessary commercial and financial acumen to turn this apparent market success into real shareholder value? For instance, Amazon's 1999 accounts contain a very long list of major uncertainties – but there is very little mention of countermeasures to deal with them.

Amazon's total market capitalization has ranged between $5bn and $10bn over the years, although not recently. This is hard to square with the above analysis of the company's growth drivers, both external and internal, which are uncertain, and with the longer-term competitive structure of the industry, which is a tough one.

Amazon provides a startling example of how growth can actually destroy rather than create shareholder value, underlying the need to seek value-based, sustainable growth. The impact of growth on the company's value and cost drivers must therefore be thought through (see Chapter 8). Without this, the potential for economic profit may not be challenged, and unsustainable and value-destroying growth might result. Amazon highlights the need to pursue a balance of growth objectives rather than too narrow a set (like market share).

This brief analysis also suggests a number of potentially fruitful lines of enquiry (possibly 'breakthroughs') for Amazon, including:

- a move up-market into Internet-based sales of higher value and higher-margin products and services;

- reducing costs in the core business to improve margins, and repackaging and repositioning its pricing and the service offering so as to capture more value and increase margins; and

- resetting expectations of future earnings with key external and internal stakeholders to more realistic levels.

Amazon highlighted the need for balanced growth, which is a very important theme in this book. To see how balanced your growth is, give your business a score across a number of key growth dimensions in the balanced growth card shown in Table 1.3.

**Table 1.3**  The balanced growth card.

| Strategic innovation | Very strong 5 | Strong 4 | Average 3 | Weak 2 | Very weak 1 |
|---|---|---|---|---|---|
| Marketing | | | | | |
| Product development | | | | | |
| Product delivery | | | | | |
| Financial planning and control | | | | | |
| Organizational capability and flexibility | | | | | |
| IT systems | | | | | |
| Total score | | | | | |

As a more refined approach to the balanced growth card, each heading can be tailored more specifically to a particular business context.

Following our initial analysis of the growth gap, we now turn to growth strategy.

## Growth strategy and the 'cunning plan'

Strategy is an often misunderstood concept. Often confused with strategic objectives, strategy is about both the 'what' and the 'how' of achieving objectives (the 'why'). Strategy has been defined (as we saw earlier) as the 'how' of moving from where we are now to where we need/want to be in the future, with competitive advantage. But whilst being fully accurate conceptually, this definition may not be terribly inspirational. For a more imaginative leap into strategic thinking, we need two further possible definitions.

- strategy is what you really, really want – and how you will get it. This is sometimes known as the 'Spice Girls strategy', after their hit single 'Wannabe'.

- strategy is the 'cunning plan'.

One of the most crucial competencies of a business leader is that of being innovative or, dare we say it, 'cunning'. And who better to turn to for an explanation of what 'cunning' really means than to Blackadder and his assistant Baldrick in the famous TV series.

"'Would you tell me please, which way I should go from here?"

"That depends a good deal on where you want to get to", said the cat.

"I don't much care where", said Alice.

"Then it doesn't matter which way you go", said the cat.'

Lewis Carroll, *Alice in Wonderland*

### *Blackadder, Baldrick and the cunning plan*

In the millennium version of *Blackadder*, Blackadder and Baldrick pilot a time machine, but unfortunately they trip on its controls, sending them back in time to various points in history. Lacking the original time co-ordinates, they begin to despair that they will ever return to the present. Blackadder laments his situation, reflecting on his fate of 'having to spend the rest of my life sharing two toilets and one room with the most stupid man on earth', i.e. Baldrick.

Baldrick, unfazed by this insult, tells Blackadder that he has an idea – which could turn out to be 'a cunning plan'. Blackadder listens intently to Baldrick's idea, which is that if Blackadder's head were held in a bucket of water to the point of drowning, and if he could be caught just at his very last moment, then when his life flashed before him he would suddenly remember the original time co-ordinates. This truly was a 'cunning plan'.

Blackadder then proceeds to upstage Baldrick by saying, 'A cunning plan, Baldrick, but even better with one little, minor modification ...' Blackadder punches Baldrick unconscious and it is Baldrick who is half-drowned to the point at which he remembers the original time co-ordinates, and they return successfully to the present.

THE 'CUNNING PLAN'

- It avoids average thinking.
- It looks at a problem in a new way.
- It sets its goals very high.
- It is obsessively innovative – and in an extremely relevant way.

The point of this story is that a 'cunning plan' has the following characteristics.

- It is absolutely not an 'average plan' (which is what most companies actually have).

- Generally, it contains some highly innovative thinking, together with some element of surprise.

- It brings together different elements, to add disproportionate value. For example, the fact that just before death, so it is claimed, an individual can remember everything in his life, and thus resolve the predicament that Blackadder and Baldrick found themselves in.

- Even when it is a cunning plan, it is open to being made better – as it was by Blackadder – into a 'stunning-plan'.

## The growth cycle

Companies and the individual business units within them typically go through a series of stages of development. Whilst there are a number of ways of understanding company life-cycles (see Fig. 1.2), the following phases do appear to be helpful.

- Vision.

- Launch.

- Development.

- Exploitation.

- Review.

- Change.

In the vision phase, managers begin to turn ideas for growth – and hopefully real inspiration – from bright ideas into a workable business model. The degree of refinement of this model, and its flexibility, will vary from case to case. It is always useful to pilot the idea before any major roll-out.

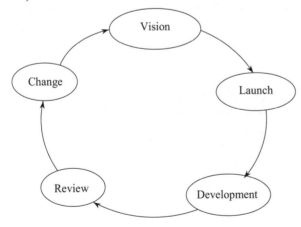

**Fig. 1.2** The growth cycle.

During launch (start-up and penetration), the business model (of how the business adds value) is put into action. In development, the business model is refined and/or replicated, resulting in expansion of operations, and frequently in an extension in market-scope. In the exploitation phase, the business ruthlessly pursues its value-creating activities within the business model. Value created is then mined, or harvested, in earnest.

In the review phase, there is a period of growing reappraisal of the business's direction and position. This can be protracted and involve a number of planning cycles and ongoing changes within top management. Ironically, little action may come out of this phase. But if the company delays its thinking (and subsequent change) for too long, then the competitive effect can be devastating (as at Marks & Spencer between 1998 and 2000).

Frequent (and minor) changes to the organizational structure are symptoms of being caught at the review stage – and not moving on into necessary change.

In the change phase, there are major shifts in the focus – and this applies to both existing and new businesses. Ailing businesses may be sold or closed down, whilst investment is steered very much towards (hopefully) new avenues of growth.

Clearly, the cycle may repeat itself with new vision being born, thus making the transition back into the initial phase (see Fig. 1.2).

The significance of the growth cycle is that:

- companies may fail to make a successful transition between one phase and another;

- some may become prematurely old, and may need to go back to the first three phases to rejuvenate themselves; and

- the company may need to adapt its management style, skills and mindset to a new stage of growth.

## Growth strategies and the strategy mix

Growth strategies come in more than one form. Not all of them are work-designed, totally clear at the outset, or are mutually consistent. Mintzberg calls these strategies 'deliberate'. Many of them are more fluid, ambiguous and disconnected. Mintzberg calls these forms of growth strategies 'emergent'. Indeed, at one point he even ventures to define strategy as 'a pattern in a series of decisions or actions.'[1]

In some ways, emergent strategies are thus akin to driving your car after it has snowed, by peering through a small hole in the snow in your windscreen to see where you are going. Your rear windscreen is completely clear (as the

'Ask anyone, planner or otherwise, "What is strategy?", and you will almost certainly be told that: (a) strategy is a plan, or something equivalent – a direction, a guide or course of action into the future, a path to get from here to there, etc. Then ask that person to describe the strategy that their organization or a competitive one has actually pursued over the past five years, and you will find that most people are perfectly happy to answer that question, oblivious to the fact that it violates their very own definition of the term. It turns out that strategy is one of those words that we inevitably define in one way yet often use in another; and (b) strategy is also a pattern, that is, consistency in behaviour over time.'

Henry Mintzberg

*Smart quotes*

snow has blown off), allowing you to see where you have been, but very little of where you are actually going.

Whilst Mintzberg's extension of the types of strategy from one to two (deliberate and now emergent) is laudable, these two forms simply do not go far enough. We have therefore added three additional forms – the 'submergent', the 'emergency' and the 'detergent' – giving:

- deliberate;

- emergent;

- submergent;

- emergency; and

- detergent.

These forms of strategy are depicted in Fig. 1.3, which shows a deliberate strategy at the start, often moving into an emergent phase. Unless its duration and implementation is steered, it may drift into a submergent or emergency phase, or even a detergent phase (where it is tidied up).

An emergency strategy is one where there is so little coherence to action that there is no real sense of direction at all. A detergent strategy is one where a strategy that has not worked in the past is now being rethought, and its various non-working parts are being discarded, or changed.[2]

Any strategy can be analysed to discern which stage of its evolution it is presently at. A strategy which is in two or more of the above phases simul-

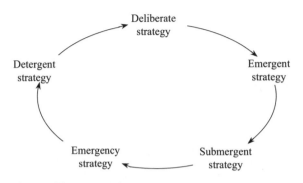

**Fig. 1.3** The strategy mix.

taneously is said to have a 'strategy mix'. This strategy mix may change considerably over time.

The strategy mix can be used for diagnosis at a number of levels – for example, for growth breakthroughs at the corporate strategy level, the business strategy level or the level of a specific growth breakthrough itself. A further explanation of each strategy type follows.

### Deliberate strategy

A deliberate strategy is one which has a very clearly formulated idea of how to get from A to B. Deliberate strategies, if innovative and skilfully crafted, can offer a more direct route to your strategic objective for growth. The proviso here is that any deliberate strategy needs to anticipate both pending external change and the complexities of implementation. Dyson (see Chapter 3) and Manchester United (see Chapter 5) are examples of deliberate growth strategies which have been successful in the past.

### Emergent strategy

An emergent strategy is one which is hard to detect as an explicit strategy at the time. Emergent strategies are more commonly ones whose pattern can only be detected after the event, once the pattern has been knitted together.

### Submergent strategy

A submergent strategy is one which was originally either a deliberate strategy which has gone wrong or an emergent strategy which has got itself into real trouble.

### Emergency strategy

Emergency strategies are characterized by having very little in the way of a longer-term pattern of strategies, being mainly reactions to short-term pressures or temptations. Emergency strategies are 'off the highway' of achieving your longer-term growth direction.

### Detergent strategy

A detergent growth strategy is often called a 'refocusing' strategy. The notion of detergent strategy is perhaps more powerful as it links directly to cleaning up a mess left after an emergent, submergent or emergency strategy.

A key conclusion from the notion of the strategy mix is that no single form of strategy is appropriate to managing strategies in different growth contexts. Deliberate, emergent and even detergent strategies need to be managed together in a deliberate juggling act. Which state is one of your own company's strategies in, and is this really appropriate? What might it cost (now or in the future) for it to remain like this?

The above forms of growth strategy are all extremely important to growth breakthroughs, as the strategy mix may be predominately one of an emergent, submergent or emergency nature. Many growth breakthroughs thus lack sufficient clarity of purpose and inherent advantage to actually succeed.

## Routes to growth

With businesses of all sizes facing competitive change in the 2000s, the pressures to find effective routes to corporate growth have intensified considerably. The mindset is often one of continual growth, rather than selective growth coupled with an ongoing review of opportunities to divest. Some corporations, however, view their portfolio more like a deck of cards representing their various growth strategies, which they can shuffle in order to generate sustainable increases in shareholder value. All businesses can learn from this approach.

Consider now the case of Virgin, which has skilfully timed its entry and exit decisions to maximize shareholder value on the route to growth.

### Virgin Group – from pop to planes to phones

To begin with, here is a brief overview of Virgin's development.

- Virgin is no longer in the pop music business, having sold its recording and publishing businesses to EMI in the mid-1990s.

- Virgin entered the airline industry in the early to mid-1990s to capitalize on the complacency of other major airlines.

- Virgin sold 49% of its share in Virgin Atlantic to Singapore Airlines at what would seem a very timely moment in the late 1990s.

- Virgin went into cinemas in the early 1990s and sold that business in 1999.

- Virgin entered financial services in 1997, then divested part of its business to Royal Bank of Scotland for around £100mn in 2001.

- Virgin entered the mobile telephone market in 1999.

The corporate mobility of the Virgin Group could be likened to a kind of 'Tarzan' strategy. Here, the critical success factor is always to grab the correct next rope in the trees to swing from, simultaneously letting go of the last one as it weakens. One moral of this is that developing or acquiring a business may not be forever – it may be appropriate only for a particular period of time. A second moral is that divestment is always a potential option – a particular business unit might be worth more (in either real or perceived terms) to a different corporate parent, who could grow it better or who has a different perception of its future growth potential.

So, to begin with, in Fig. 1.4 we see the three major routes to corporate growth as being:

- alliances;

- organic development; and

- acquisitions.

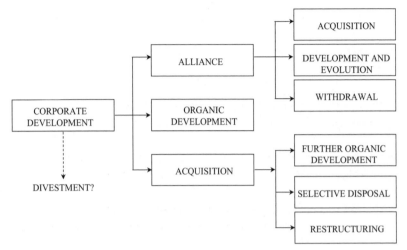

Fig. 1.4  Routes to corporate growth.

But notice how each route then branches off into sub-options. Thus, alliances can lead to acquisition, development or withdrawal (i.e. divestment). Equally, acquisition can lead to further organic development or selective disposal, or to restructuring. Growth strategy therefore ought to be very much a 'mix and match' process, bearing in mind: the changing environment; competitive opportunities; and your own competencies and resources. Above all, we should ask the key questions, 'What do we want to achieve through our strategy?' and 'What strategic options are available and which adds most/least shareholder value?', rather than 'Who should we jump into bed with (i.e. acquire or have an alliance with)?'

One particularly enticing route for growth is that of acquisitions, which we now explore.

*Acquisitions – the good and the bad*

There are a number of good and not-so-good reasons for making acquisitions. The good reasons are:

- to gain genuine and tangible economies of scale which will manifest themselves in lower internal or bought-in costs;

- to take out corporate and business overhead which is adding little value or which can easily be substituted by your own resource; and

- to acquire a particular product or set of services that can easily be sold through your own distribution channels and without significant operational or organizational distraction.

The not-so-good reasons for acquiring businesses are:

- to acquire market share, but where market-share increases will not necessarily result in gains in shareholder value;

- to establish a presence in a market which is booming, but only at the moment;

- in response to the fact that competitors are themselves acquiring, when they may be foolishly doing so;

- as a defensive measure (unless all other defensive options have been explored and exhausted – and even then if, and only if, it is better to stay in the business longer-term rather than to exit);

- to satisfy the expectations of the stock market, which is expecting you to make a move of this kind;

- for a new management leader or team to be seen as having done something significant, big and bold within the first 12 to 18 months; and

- to further your own (or the team's) personal career aspirations and/or agendas as a primary purpose.

The sheer number of not-so-good reasons for acquiring underlines the importance of examining why it is – *precisely* – that you might wish to acquire a business.

On average, acquisitions tend to destroy rather than add to shareholder value.[3] It is invariably an uphill battle to generate shareholder value through acquisition, as any company that is strong and/or has lots of future potential will typically be prohibitively expensive. Also, the buyer is likely to have far more imperfect data on the business than the seller. Sadly, in general terms (except in a forced sale), divestment tends to generate superior shareholder value relative to an acquisition.

Table 1.4 below gives some perceived advantages and disadvantages of different routes to corporate growth to be borne in mind before going down the acquisition route.

But we can question this table on the following grounds. First, organic growth is often not perceived as being as exciting as other forms of corporate development – and, of course, it is slower. But whilst it does take some time to develop a company organically, the speed with which agile companies can move organically is often impressive. Organic growth can be a lot faster than managers might perceive it can be. It can also then surprise competitors and put them off their balance. Consider the speed with which, amongst several other product innovations, Tesco exploited its non-food products and Internet-based Homeshopping scheme in the late 1990s.

**Table 1.4** Routes to growth.

| | Organic growth | Acquisitions | Alliances/joint ventures |
|---|---|---|---|
| Advantages | Easier to control. Builds around core competencies. Lower risk. | Fast. Extends competencies and opportunities. Surprises competitors. | Opens exciting new opportunities. Transcends limited competencies. Surprises competitors. |
| Disadvantages | Slower. May involve up-front revenue costs. Unlikely to surprise competitors. | Costly. Difficult and potentially risky. Hits profits. Time-consuming. | Alliance may crumble. Collaborators may dominate. Doesn't give control. Perceived lower-quality earnings. |

Whilst acquisitions may well be fast to target, negotiate and do the deal, successful integration may take longer than expected. And success could be elusive – far from being fast, it can be extremely slow indeed, as our case on BMW's acquisition of Rover illustrates (see Chapter 4).

Acquisitions that prove very difficult can not only absorb a lot of scarce senior management time (and thus destroy value) through opportunity cost, but can also detract from other value-creating activities, especially those coming from organic growth, alliances (which might sometimes achieve strategic goals more effectively and at lower cost), and maintaining and protecting core operations.

## *The growth process and techniques*

Growth is not merely something that happens – it is a process. This process is shown in Fig. 1.5, and breaks down into:

- diagnosing growth;

**Fig. 1.5** Managing the growth process.

- creating growth options;

- evaluating growth options;

- implementing growth; and

- learning and control.

Diagnosing growth introduces us to:

- external growth drivers;

- internal growth drivers; and

- the five competitive forces (Chapter 2).

Creating growth options brings in:

- the industry mindset (Chapter 2);

- scenarios and uncertainty grids (Chapter 3);

- the octopus grid (Chapter 3);

- wishbone analysis (Chapter 3).

Evaluating growth options focuses on:

- the strategic option grid (Chapter 3);

- the GE grid (Chapter 3);

- uncertainty grid (Chapter 2);

- value and cost drivers (Chapter 8);

- force-field analysis (Chapter 7); and

- stakeholder analysis (Chapter 7).

Implementing growth focuses on:

- fishbone analysis;

- attractiveness/implementation-difficulty (AID) analysis;

- force-field analysis;

- the difficulty-over-time curve; and

- stakeholder (and stakeholder agenda) analysis (Chapter 7).

Learning and control looks principally at:

- uncertainty and importance/influence grids (Chapter 2);

- wishbone analysis (Chapter 3);

- fishbone analysis (Chapter 7); and

- value and cost drivers (Chapter 8).

Notice that a number of the techniques are used at more than one stage of the overall process. For example, fishbone analysis (a technique from Total Quality Management) is used to plan the implementation process and also during learning and change. Equally, the uncertainty grid is used during the process of creating growth options and also in the learning and control phase.

Using these techniques will greatly speed up group-working on growth strategies – and will reduce frustration.

### *Smart working – strategic thinking techniques and organizational speed*

The senior managers at a major financial services company's IT department met to spend a one-day workshop to diagnose IT strategic projects and to prioritize them. Using the 'AID' analysis – on the attractiveness/implementation-difficulty grid (see Chapter 3) – they were able to prioritize key projects in just one day. Afterwards, one of the their managers reflected:

*'Well, we would not have done that in anything like a day in our normal management mode. It would probably have taken five days to get that far ... no, actually, thinking about it, we would never have actually got there.'*

Sometimes the techniques can be used on a stand-alone basis. For example, when diagnosing a growth constraint it may be sufficient to use fishbone analysis alone. On other occasions, perhaps two or three techniques would be used in succession, perhaps along the following lines.

- What are the root causes of a current growth constraint? (Fishbone analysis – see Chapter 3).

- How can we tackle these, and with what priority? (AID analysis – see Chapter 3).

- How difficult would these be to implement? (Force-field analysis and the difficulty-over-time curve – see Chapter 7).

### *An overview of the book*

In Chapter 2 we look at understanding the context for growth. This entails examining the external growth drivers within your markets – those external factors which dynamically increase the physical size and/or value of the market. The internal growth drivers which affect an individual business's ability to grow are then explored.

We then turn to the five competitive forces that determine the level of competitive pressure in a market. These include: the bargaining power of buyers and of suppliers; entry barriers; substitutes; and rivalry. A key theme is also that of the industry mindset, which underpins the competitive behaviour within a market. This is illustrated with the unusual (but strangely humorous) case study of the funerals industry, which is now becoming an international industry. We then explore the use of scenarios to anticipate future growth – and especially the application of uncertainty grids to help understand discontinuity.

In Chapter 3 we turn to the diagnosis of growth issues at a business level. Taking the growth constraints identified in Chapter 2, we diagnose these using fishbone analysis. We then look at how to scope a growth opportunity – and to align it to your vision for growth – with wishbone analysis and through considering the Dyson Appliances case.

In Chapter 4 we look at one more creative side of growth strategy, especially through the notion of growth breakthroughs (the Japanese philosophy of *hoshin*). By creating lines of enquiry for growth (the 'Lieutenant Columbo' approach), we generate creative options for growth.

Once we have generated some fruitful options, we then show how they can be evaluated using the strategic option grid – both on a top-down and on a bottom-up basis (i.e. through using further analysis techniques). We then use these techniques to illustrate the attractiveness of BMW's strategic options and of its cross-border acquisition of Rover Group.

Chapter 5 takes a specific look at organic routes to growth, beginning with a look at how, in practice, effective growth strategies can be devised, and giving tips on facilitation. We then turn to organizational growth, examining how organizational capability needs to be developed in order to promote and sustain growth. This leads on to a major case study on Manchester United Football Club and the football industry, in which we investigate growth trends, and look at future growth prospects and some specific options for Manchester United.

In Chapter 6 we take a more detailed look at acquisitions as a route to growth. This is then illustrated with the classic case study of Granada versus Forte, with both companies' management teams competing to achieve value-led growth for Forte's business portfolio.

Chapter 7 then takes us, step-by-step, through a process for implementing growth strategies. This process has been proven at major companies, including, for example, Nokia, Microsoft, Standard Life and Tesco. Here, we look at how implementation of growth strategies can be project managed, and also at how change issues can be anticipated and overcome.

In Chapter 8 we turn to the vexed problem of putting a value on growth strategies. We examine the three 'curses' of value – interdependencies, intangibles and uncertainty. We then use value and cost drivers to link growth strategy with growth value, as input into the business case.

Chapter 9 contains some practical (and exhaustive) checklists for managing growth, including organic growth, acquisitions, alliances, franchises, international development, the Internet and organizational capability.

Finally, in Chapter 10, we summarize the key lessons of the book and make some suggestions for further action. This includes a most useful and practical section on 'growing your own career'.

To recap, the goals of this book are to:

- give you more of a helicopter view of the issues which are involved in managing growth;

- show you how a process can be used to manage these issues more effectively;

- introduce you to some practical techniques which you can use at an everyday level;

- give you some chances to apply them, both through the case studies and also with some of your own issues; and

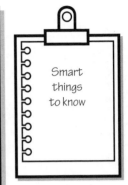

Smart things to know

1 Growth depends on determination and reinvention – the Madonna approach.
2 Growth requires objectives – which need to be spelt out and prioritized.
3 Successful growth typically focuses on a small number of strategic breakthroughs.
4 An effective strategy must have a 'cunning plan'.
5 Growth strategies require a gap analysis.
6 Growth strategies come in a number of forms, which comprise the 'strategy mix'.
7 Growth follows a cycle that needs to be understood and managed.
8 Growth requires a deliberate process.
9 There are a range of paths to growth – including organic growth, acquisition and alliances – the benefits and costs of which need to be fully thought through.

- build your confidence to the point where you can make your next career step as a senior business manager.

## Notes

1 Mintzberg, H. (1994) *The Rise and Fall of Strategic Planning*. Prentice Hall, Hemel Hempstead.

2 See: Grundy, A.N. (1995) *Breakthrough Strategies for Growth*. Pitman Publishing, London.

3 Porter, E.M. (1987) 'From Competitive Advantage to Corporate Strategy'. *Harvard Business Review*, pp. 43–59, May–June.

# 2
# Managing Growth Drivers and Competitive Pressure

## Introduction

In this chapter we first examine the external growth drivers which shape the past, current and future growth of the external market. We then look at the internal growth drivers (and brakes) which determine its capability to create and to digest growth. Next, we consider the five competitive forces and the industry mindset, which largely determines the quality of external growth (as opposed to its quantity). This is then illustrated with a case study on the funerals industry. Finally, we show how scenarios can help us to anticipate the future environment more easily, and we then use two forms of the uncertainty grid to focus on key vulnerabilities.

## External growth drivers

Growth drivers that are inherent in the external market can include a variety of things, as shown in the following examples.

- Service innovation – a new market (or segment) may be more attractive to customers than the existing one, because the need is now delivered in a cheaper and/or better way. For example, telephone or Internet banking and telephone insurance might offer customers a cheaper or better service (or, arguably, both) than existing, more expensive or inflexible, providers.

- Technology innovation – a new technology (for instance, mobile telephones or personal computers) may enable the customer to satisfy previously unserved needs or ones which were at best inconveniently served in the past.

- Increased learning about products or services – there may be an increase in awareness among customers that the product or service exists, and as to how its benefits can be extracted. Once customers have learned more about these benefits, this is likely to increase the frequency of usage.

- Price reductions – as a market expands, growth can feed on itself as companies gain economies of scale. The benefits of these economies are then passed on to the customer in the form of lower prices. These lower prices can then induce penetration of new customers and/or increase frequency of purchase. (Or a single competitor might break rank and reduce its prices, causing a surge in demand and increasing its own market share.)

*Growing the airline market – the 'easy' (Jet) way*

In the mid-1990s, Stelios (as he prefers to be known) launched the new airline easyJet, to focus on simplifying the airline market for short trips. By focusing on delivering superior value for money for customers (with flights as cheap as £30), Stelios stimulated demand, and created virtually a new market segment. Joined by British Airways subsidiary, Go, and a number of smaller rivals, Stelios capitalized on the increasing income of the late 1990s and the boom in tourism. Stelios's innovation in the industry become not merely an internal growth driver (helping his airline to grow), but also helped the overall market itself to grow.

Growth drivers are those factors which actually influence the growth in aggregate market demand. To maintain the purity of the techniques, external growth-driver analysis should not embrace internal growth drivers and brakes – not simultaneously at least. The key reasons for this are that:

- it is likely that your analysis will then divert too much towards internal thinking; and

- the resulting analysis will be less helpful for external market forecasting, as you will now have a mix between external and internal growth drivers.

Internal growth drivers should therefore be analysed separately (as we see in the next section).

The growth drivers do not merely tease out forces impacting on volume, but also those impacting on value. One can easily be faced with a situation of a market experiencing good volume-growth, but with prices (in real terms) coming down. This may either slow market growth considerably or possibly even make the market shrink.

Besides its use for business analysis, growth drivers can be used for understanding the sustainability of internal business expansion – which may be fuelling your job security and promotion opportunities. When taking a new job, think carefully about the strength and sustainability of the growth drivers impacting on business demand.

Once all the key growth drivers within the market have been identified, it is essential to evaluate their combined effect. Here, a pictorial representation of the overall growth drivers provides stimulus for debate. This is accomplished through vector analysis, where arrows are used to represent the strength of growth drivers and the length of the vector arrow represents the perceived strength of the force driving growth.

Taking a graphic example of growth drivers, let us examine the growth in the price of dot.com shares in 1998–9. Here, the main growth drivers were:

- the huge growth in usage of the Internet (during 1997–9);

- the perceived possibilities for reducing costs and thus reducing price (as at Amazon.com); and

- media hype.

The rise in dot.com share prices began to feed on itself, creating a self-fulfilling prophecy. Also, this became an 'emperor's clothes syndrome' – no one appeared willing to question the fundamental economic logic of this boom.

The growth drivers of dot.com share prices are shown in Fig. 2.1 (as at 1998–9). But by mid-2000 through to 2001, sentiment had reversed. It would appear that the growth in Internet use was perhaps a necessary – but not a sufficient – condition of revenue and margin generation. What was also needed to sustain both market and share price growth was:

- a preparedness by customers to make transactions through the Internet (either directly or indirectly – i.e. via Internet advertising);

- that this demand was actually both massive and reasonably profitable; and

- the dot.com companies that had been set up would be well-managed and be able to deliver real shareholder value – not so much later, but preferably sooner (or at least 'soon-ish').

The conditions were not met – big-time.

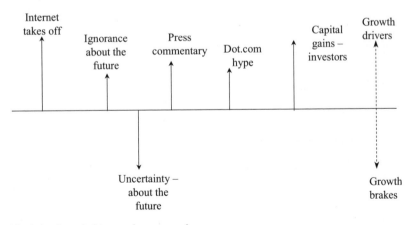

**Fig. 2.1**   Growth drivers – dot.com market.

Figure 2.2 plots the new growth drivers (and brakes) in late 2000 through to mid-2001. The growth in Internet usage takes on a much lesser and weaker importance. The mounting losses of dot.com companies (and in many cases the sheer absence of revenues) reversed sentiment. Once this rot in sentiment had set in, it became a disastrous self-fulfilling prophecy.

In conclusion, growth drivers are an essential tool for thinking strategically about the external market. Many managers find growth-driver analysis actually easier to use than Porter's five competitive forces (coming soon) and actually use it more frequently.

To summarize, growth-driver analysis helps you to:

- identify possibilities for actively influencing the growth of the market, rather than just being passive;

- do a reality-check on assumptions of future market growth; and

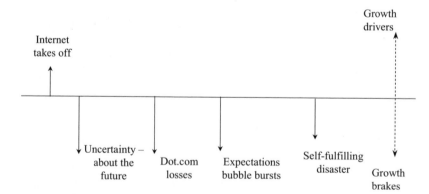

**Fig. 2.2** New growth drivers – dot.com market.

- be more objective about potential 'exit' decisions from specific markets, by checking out whether assumed growth in a market is a reality or merely a mirage.

## Internal growth drivers

Internal growth drivers are those internal factors within the organization which either enable it to grow or may constrain its growth. Internal growth drivers might include, for example:

- excellent quality products;

- responsive service;

- management capability; and

- sufficient financial resources.

Examples of internal growth brakes would include:

- senior management's mindset;

- over-restrictive budgeting processes;

- excessive organizational politics; and

- management succession constraints.

## Internal growth drivers at Belgo's

Around 1997, the Belgo restaurant in London's Covent Garden – part of the international restaurant group – was acquired by outside investors, who grew the business by opening other Belgo restaurants in the UK, Ireland and elsewhere in Europe, and in the US.

Belgo's format was to serve Belgian beers and hearty meals in a frenetically busy environment. A novelty was that the waiters were dressed as Belgian monks. Queues to eat in Belgos can reach one hour on a Saturday night, such is the popularity of its Covent Garden restaurant. This restaurant is reputed to be the busiest restaurant in Britain.

Featured by the television programme *Trouble at the Top* in 2000, one of the investors in Belgo's spent a week learning the ropes in his own restaurant. Not only did he find this a most difficult and taxing experience, but he discovered (see Fig. 2.3) some major internal growth brakes at Belgo's.

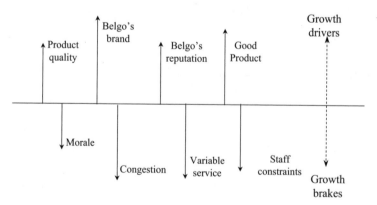

**Fig. 2.3**   Internal growth drivers at Belgo's restaurant.

The internal growth drivers should be analysed separately from the external growth drivers. Beware of their specific focus on *growth* – this analysis is invariably more powerful and insightful than a SWOT analysis.

## Uncertainty grids and scenarios

Turning now to uncertainty, we look at two versions of the uncertainty grid, which allows us to test the robustness of growth strategies. We then look at the use of growth scenarios, which can help us to (in effect) begin to see around corners into the future.

One way of testing the external and internal assumptions underpinning a strategy is by using a qualitative importance–uncertainty grid (see Fig. 2.4) (derived from Mitroff & Linstone (1993)). Using this grid, managers can plot the key assumptions driving the value of any strategic decision. These can be external and internal, and include 'soft' as well as 'hard' assumptions.

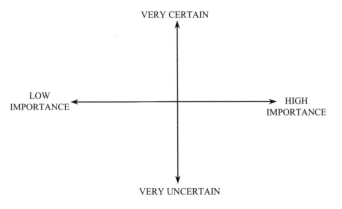

> *Smart quotes*
>
> 'There are two certainties in life – death and taxes. But whilst taxes have certain timing, death's timing is uncertain, but you can still take out a strategic pre-need plan before you actually become deceased …'

**Fig. 2.4** Importance–uncertainty grid.

Having selected a subset of these assumptions, these are then prioritized by using the grid (which can be on a flipchart, a whiteboard, or simply a piece of paper). Once assumptions have been carefully and skilfully defined, it is possible to debate their relative importance and uncertainty (using a flip-chart, the assumptions can be moved around easily using self-adhesive notes).

These assumptions are defined in terms of 'the future world being OK'. For example, if we were using it to understand the uncertainties of getting to a meeting in Amsterdam on time, one assumption would be defined as 'the easyJet *will* run on time', and not 'the easyJet will *not* run on time'.

A frequent mistake (when first using the grid) is to have some assumptions defined positively and some negatively. This makes it impossible to judge the overall downsides to a strategy. An example of this would be the following scenario.

- 'There will be a hold-up on the M1 (on the way to Luton airport) of over 30 minutes' (a post-negative assumption).

- 'Kings Cross Station might be closed' (a negative assumption).

- 'There will be no delays on the motorway of more than 30 minutes' (a positive assumption).

Instead, please frame each assumption in a positive way.

At the beginning of the appraisal of a growth strategy, key assumptions are likely to be mapped in the due-north and north-east quadrants (as moderate-to-high importance, and of low uncertainty). Upon testing, it is quite common to find one or more assumptions moving over to the danger zone in the south-east (that is, of high importance and high uncertainty).

Figure 2.5 shows a growth strategy which entails a new product launch. The extra sales volume from existing customers is very important, but also considered relatively certain. Sales to new customers are considerably more uncertain (but also very important). These are shown in the south-east of the grid. Product launch costs are somewhat less important and also reasonably certain (shown just slightly north-east of the centre of the grid).

Interestingly, a more fundamental assumption is that competitors will not imitate with a better product in the second year. In this case, the assumption is shown as beginning life just west of the assumption as to product launch costs (relatively certain and less important), but is actually heading south-east.

Besides the appraisal itself, the uncertainty grid is also helpful for targeting data collection on growth strategies. Data collection efforts should be aimed at learning more about those assumptions that are either most

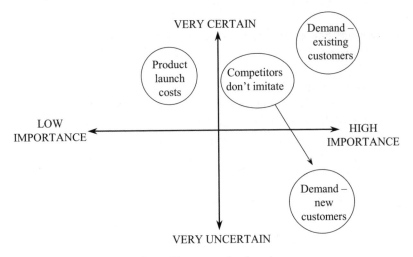

**Fig. 2.5** Importance–uncertainty grid – new product launch.

important or most uncertain, or both, and not those of data which is just easier to collect. The uncertainty and importance grid is also a vital tool for evaluating assumptions prior to undertaking any financial sensitivities. This tool helps focus these sensitivities towards the most critical uncertainties (for example, to the possibility of new competitor entry).

The uncertainty grid is often misunderstood by managers for a number of reasons, including the following.

- Their mindset is one of putting on the grid what they will actually do to achieve the strategy. Whilst it is perfectly possible to use the grid in this way, when we are conducting preliminary strategic analysis, this would be inappropriate and premature. Instead, position the *assumptions* on the grid.

- Managers are not used to thinking explicitly about their assumptions, as these are often taken for granted.

- Managers find it very hard to think about the future, let alone to creatively imagine it.

The uncertainty grid can be used either before implementing a growth strategy, during implementation, or for its post-review. Here, assumptions that were previously implicit often crystallize in a startling and unexpected way – whether becoming most important or most uncertain.

The uncertainty grid can also be used for:

- new market entry;

- product development;

- diversification;

- investment decisions;

- acquisitions and alliances;

- business reappraisal and turnaround;

- e-commerce strategies; and

- last but not least, developing a strategy for your own career.

The key benefits of the uncertainty grid are that:

- it helps to identify the vulnerabilities and blind-spots in a strategy;

- it helps managers to focus on the future, rather than on the present; and

- its simple format allows it to be used at a very intuitive level – so that paper representation is not really essential.

As with many analysis techniques, it can give you the illusion of comfort, when that is inappropriate. To test this out, it can be extremely helpful to also ask a final question: 'What is the one BIG THING we have missed?' – this will help to cover blind-spots.

KILLER QUESTIONS

What is not just the one BIG THING we have missed, but also the second BIG THING we have missed?

An associated grid is the uncertainty–influence grid (Fig. 2.6). Here, the horizontal axis is low uncertainty through to high uncertainty, but the vertical axis represents low influence through to high influence. Again we plot on the grid the key assumptions of the future turning out right,

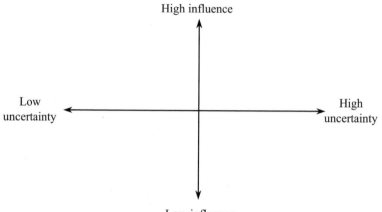

**Fig. 2.6** Uncertainty–influence grid.

not wrong. The danger zone here reflects those assumptions which are both most uncertain and over which we have low influence.

Once we have identified the respective positionings, we then:

- focus corrective action on those areas which are most uncertain but over which we have greatest influence; and

- focus our creative thinking on those areas which are most uncertain and over which we have least influence (through developing the 'cunning plan' and through the search for options for growth described in Chapter 4).

Uncertainty can also be explored using scenarios – which are 'stories about the future' about how growth will emerge in that specific future. Scenarios have been well-popularized for many years (particularly by Shell managers and by other planners), but for many the purpose of scenario development appears unclear.

The key questions that are now addressed are as follows.

- What are scenarios?

- How can scenarios help?

- How can scenarios be developed – and quickly?

Scenarios:

- are internally consistent views of the future;

- focus on discontinuity and change (not on continuity);

- involve exploring how the underlying systems in the business environment may generate change; and

- are views of how the competitive players (existing and new) might behave.

Scenarios are not static or comprehensive views of the future. They are, in many ways, more like a video film – they are of necessity selective, but contain a dynamic story-line. Scenarios thus contain a series of views (pictures) of the future. This is fruitfully presented as a series of pictures, not as a single one, but there is also a storyline which enables these pictures to hang together.

Just as strategy is frequently defined as a pattern in a stream of (past and current) decisions, so a scenario is a pattern of future events, and of the interaction between customers, competitors and other key players in the industry. The scenario story can be run (again like a video film) forwards or backwards. By replaying the story, you can work backwards from a particular scenario to see what events might bring about a particular outcome. (These events are called 'transitional events'.)

Next, although many managers understand change, they are frequently bemused by the idea of 'discontinuity'. Discontinuity simply means a major break between past and future. Discontinuity can occur imperceptibly – for example, just as a train may be switched from one line to another. Or it can happen abruptly – with a big jolt, as in the 2001 terrorist attack on New York's World Trade Center.

Scenarios naturally involve in-depth thinking about how the external environment actually works. For example, how might a change in regulation bring about market growth, changes in prices and margins, the levels of competitive rivalry and the pattern of competitor dominance? This implies looking at industry dynamics, the impact of lags in the market (for instance, in recognition of what is going on and subsequent behaviour). In Ansoff's terms (1975), they are ways of picking up, amplifying and interpreting weak signals in the environment.

Scenarios are *not*:

- mere forecasts;

- projections from past trends;

- fixed or rigid world-views;

- complete in all details; or

- static.

Scenarios can help in a number of ways. Scenario planning at Shell is principally known for its very 'big picture' analysis – particularly for global or industry-wide scenarios, or for country-specific scenarios. In addition, managers can perform issue-specific scenarios – for example, the impact of regulatory/environmental pressure – or scenarios can be created specifically for a particular growth strategy.

We now look at some examples of scenarios in practice.

## Developments in telecommunications in the mid-1990s

A major global telecommunications company wanted to explore how it might set about accelerating scenario development. The company had used scenarios to a limited extent in the past, but had found them to be slow and arduous to create. The challenge set was this: how could they create a small number of scenarios for a key market in less than a day?

A small (but hand-picked) team was assembled, which included the representatives, technical experts and planning staff. An external consultant was also included, whose task was to design and facilitate the process, not to give expert input on scenario content. Once the issue had been defined, a number of key questions aimed at probing views of the future were defined. It is also useful to have two small teams working in parallel on the scenario – with core common assumptions, but with deliberate divergence at the later stages of the process.

These were then positioned on the uncertainty–importance grid. These highlighted that:

- the impact of the Internet was both very important and very uncertain (in the mid-1990s its impact had been minuscule);

- there was a shift towards more electronically intelligent homes; and

- potentially, greater polarization between income levels in the UK could lead to increased crime and an emphasis on personal security, and in turn more focus on the home.

Whist the first two of the above assumptions were positioned in a prophetic way, the third one failed to materialize. (In this particular case the assumption was defined as: 'There will *not* be a significant rise in crime levels', and this was positioned as *both* very important and very uncertain.) But this only underlines the need to avoid trying to get the *right answer* with scenarios – their main purpose is to explore the possibilities and potential for growth in the future.

Next, the key driving systems impacting on the market environment are identified. For instance, for the do-it-yourself UK retail market (in the late 1990s) the following were identified.

- Changes in social and demographic lifestyles (e.g. the breakdown of the 'nuclear' family).

- The impact of the housing market.

- Change in leisure patterns.

- The pattern of rivalry in the marketplace (for example, now that the grocery chain Sainsbury's had bought the out-of-town DIY retailer, Texas, in the UK).

This kind of analysis is best done in a pictorial way. Figure 2.7 outlines some pictures of this industry. This highlights not merely the complexity of the external systems impacting on the industry, but also the influence of key clusters, particularly those around the housing market and the economy, family leisure patterns, and also competitive rivalry.

The scenario storyline, which was written in 1995 for the period to 2000, ran as follows.

- A Labour government gaining power, with slightly higher taxes that would erode the incomes of income-rich people, but not those of DIY fanatics in particular.

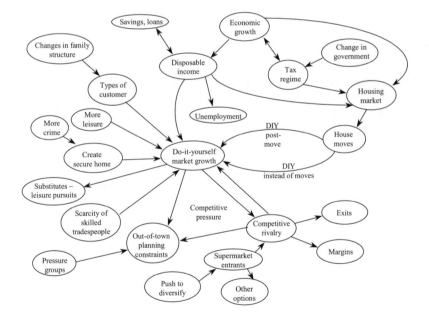

**Fig. 2.7**   Scenarios for the UK DIY markets (late 1990s).

- Reductions in unemployment, making it hard to get tradespeople to do jobs around the home at a reasonable price.

- This would lead to the dominant player [which, as it happened, turned out to be Sainsbury's] to begin to make very good profits out of DIY goods, especially as no new sites could be opened (due to planning restrictions) so profitability per outlet would go up.

A complementary approach to scenarios is to role-play your competitors (and, for that matter, other key players, like major customers, suppliers or regulatory bodies) and how they might behave in the storyline of the scenario. This helps inject more life and dynamism into the scenario picture.

### Deregulation of the UK energy industry in the mid-1990s

A US oil company, active in exploration activities in the North Sea, wanted to investigate the potential for expanding into selling gas in the UK, around the time of deregulation in the mid-1990s. A one-day scenario workshop was devised. At its centrepiece, a number of senior managers, armed with a two-page competitor profile for each of its major players, came in time to put their cards for their growth interest on the table.

The managers became very engrossed in this role-play. One person, role-playing another weak US company, mimicked: 'All this competition is too much – look, I have hurt my knee! I am off back to the US to recuperate.'

The manager playing British Gas was the star performer. He sat down in the chair and (perhaps a little unfairly) pretended to fall asleep. The team concluded that the future threat would not come from British Gas but from new entrants, like themselves.

> 'Although potentially useful, scenario planning, yields industry foresight. None of these tools compels senior management to reconceive the corporation and the industries in which it competes. Only by changing the lens through which the corporation is viewed ... only by changing the lens through which markets are viewed (functionality versus products), only by broadening the angle of the lens (becoming more inquisitive), only by cleaning off the accumulated grime on the lens (seeing with a child's eyes), only by peering through multiple lenses, and only by occasionally disbelieving what one actually sees ... can the future be anticipated.'
>
> Hamel & Prahalad

Once a small number of growth scenarios have been developed, they should be then exposed to cross-testing by the two teams. This will help to:

- reveal why particular assumptions were thought most important and most uncertain (and, conversely, why others were least important and most certain);

- draw out the implications for strategy, and for the critical success factors; and

- begin to bring out the financial implications of the scenario.

Some overall lessons from scenario development in the past are that you need to:

- bring line-managers and planners together to create scenarios;

- ensure that the scenario feeds directly into the planning and decision-making processes;

- avoid too many views of the future (preferably keep to two);

- manage concerns that 'we will never get the right [i.e. precise] answer to ...' (scenarios are not about making forecasts);

- use a few analysis tools, which also avoids lots of detailed data input and frees the mind to be creative;

- refine and revisit scenarios, especially where new signals are detected in the business environment.

The benefits of scenario development for growth strategies are thus that they:

- can help you to 'see around corners', which in turn helps you to cope with uncertainty;

- make managers more sensitive and alert to changes in their environment, both external and internal;

- make managers 'think future', in a way which conventional planning often does not; and

- encourage you to think 'how can we create a desired future?'

## The five competitive forces

The five competitive forces (Porter, 1980) provide an essential technique for analysing the quality of your past, present and future growth (see Fig. 2.8). These five competitive forces comprise:

- buyer power (i.e. that of customers);

- substitutes;

- entrants (i.e. the threat of other entrants);

- supplier power; and

- competitive rivalry (between existing players and, indeed, yourselves).

To help demystify Porter's five competitive forces, let us take a look at an industry neglected by most strategic commentators, but one ripe for transformation – funeral services.

### An unusual case study – the funeral services industry

In analysing a perhaps unusual industry – that of funerals (or, more explicitly, burials and cremations) – it can be seen that overall a relatively

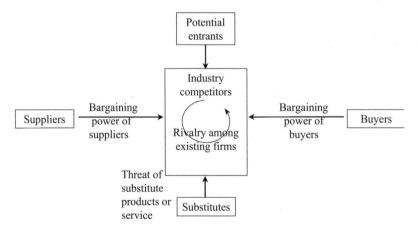

**Fig. 2.8**   Porter's five forces.

favourable picture emerges (see Fig. 2.9). The European industry is ripe for strategic breakthrough, even though the total market volume is actually decreasing (as people are living longer and longer). In the US the market has already been transformed (Grundy, 1994).

**Buyer power**
First, buyers have relatively low bargaining power. When someone dies it is usually an urgent process to sort out the funeral and other arrangements. Further, the buyer (the deceased's relatives) is in the unusual position of paying for the burial indirectly – from the deceased's estate. The buyer may also be emotionally affected by the death. The buyer is thus unlikely to be in a state of mind conducive to driving a hard bargain, shopping around or going for a lowest-cost burial, all of which might look conspicuous in front of other relatives. In short, this situation of low buyer-power is of clear advantage to players in the funeral industry.

As Jessica Mitford (a critic of the funeral industry for many years) explained on the UK's Channel 4 Television:

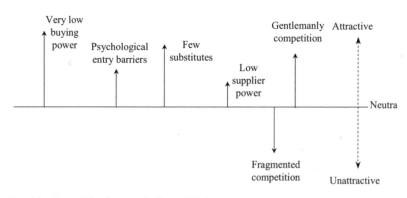

Fig. 2.9    Porter's five forces – the funerals industry.

*'The funeral transaction is unlike any other. If you buy a car or a house, you discuss it with everybody, you shop around, and you consult. But if you have got a dead body in your living room then this puts a different complexion on things. You are likely to call the first undertaker who comes to mind.*

*'Once he comes in there and gets the body, that's the end of it as far as he is concerned. In other words, you are very unlikely to insist on someone else after that.'*

### Substitutes
Second, 'substitutes' for a conventional burial in modern society have not really existed – at least in the UK (except, of course, for the option of cemetery or crematorium). The DIY burial is not socially acceptable. Substitutes are therefore relatively unimportant – currently at least.

Jane Spottiswode, author of *Undertaken with Love*, recounted (also on Channel 4) a DIY experiment with her husband's body:

*'Well, the only real difficulty was getting a coffin, because I started with local undertakers and, shock, horror, they said, "We only provide it as part of our full service."*

*'So then I tried the undertakers' suppliers, and the same thing happened. But then I found one. They thought it was a bit unusual. I got the coffin. It was chipboard and it was £36 plus VAT.*

*'Friends of mine had a Volvo, and they didn't want me to pick it up in my Mini – it wasn't quite the thing; we put it in the loft until my husband died because we knew there was no way he would live – he had lung cancer.*

*'When he died, after various tribulations, we put him in the coffin and we took it and him to the crematorium. The funeral cost us just under £200 for everything.'*

### Entrants

Third, entrants may not be attracted to the funeral industry because of its traditionally gloomy image. On the other hand, real entry barriers may not be so high, particularly where a determined player enters by acquisition (as is now happening in the UK). Acquisitions may therefore enable entry and thereby shift the entry barrier indicator from being a 'favourable' force to one which is 'slightly less favourable'.

Howard Hodgson (a former UK undertaker and now millionaire and author of *How to Get Dead Rich*) reflects on how business was done in the industry 20 years ago. This entry/acquisition strategy also yielded some very tangible economies of scale for Howard Hodgson's business. He continues:

*'It was very much a cottage industry; it was very much, other than the Co-Op, family, small. We needed to buy these [businesses] locally in order for us to have a strategy, which went from strength to strength. In fact, by 1990 we had established 546 outlets in the United Kingdom and were the largest funeral directors in the country.*

*'There were considerable economies of scale. The average family firm of funeral directors had to have a hearse, probably two limousines, and conduct five or six funerals a week. The capital equipment was used once a day. By acquiring firms in the area and rationalising, we were able to get one of these limousines to go out five or six times a day each.'*

The operational structure of a growth business will determine a good deal of the economic value which is generated. Here the number of funerals per hearse, per day is a 'cost driver' (see Chapter 8).

Besides Howard Hodgson, a major entrant is Service Corporation International (SCI) of the US. Apparently (according to Channel 4), funeral prices since SCI entered the Australian market increased by 40%. Even where pre-paid funerals are involved, this can apparently increase industry profitability, as the supplier reaps the fruit of receiving pre-paid investment funds.

The pre-need market offers potential not merely for capturing value before death, but also for value added by pre-planning tailored funerals. Apparently, in some cultures this has been the norm in the past. In China, for example, over a hundred years ago, all funerals were pre-planned, with individuals taking up to 20 years to refine the exotic details of their funeral plans (*The Mail on Sunday*, 20 May 2001). This analysis suggests a surplus of latent customer value – if only customers might begin to see preparation for a funeral as an opportunity, and not as a threat.

### Supplier power
Fourth, suppliers may have some bargaining power (especially in restricting space for graves or even for cemetery plaques), but there appears to be nothing special in the supply of hardware like coffins, hearses or the provision of flowers. This again is a favourable force, enhancing the quality of growth in this market.

### Competitive rivalry
Fifth, existing firms in the industry are currently relatively fragmented (few having significant market share, even locally against one another). Also, competitive behaviour is restrained, given the cultural norms of the industry. Thus, we would rate competitive rivalry overall as favourable, but as relatively important.

*Analysis*

So, taking the five forces as a whole (see Fig. 2.10), it can be seen that the market is currently 'favourable'. Here we use a vector analysis format (similar to the growth drivers) to do two things in one:

- to sort out whether a force is favourable (upward arrows) or unfavourable (downward arrows); and

- to prioritize its importance.

This analysis suggests that:

- if already in the industry, longer-term profit should be good (unless entrants move in and restructure the industry or buyer power strengthens);

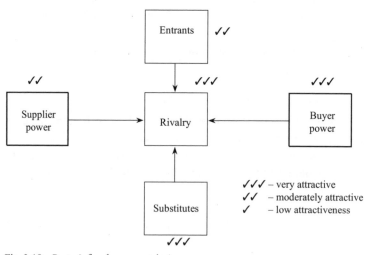

Fig. 2.10   Porter's five forces – analysis.

- if rated against other industries for identifying avenues for growth strategies, it might be considered to be an (inherently) attractive one to enter; and

- critical success factors for achieving quality growth are building one's brand (to keep entrants out) and perhaps seeking a differentiation strategy.

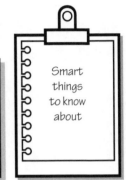

Smart things to know about

---

THE FUNERALS INDUSTRY

- It is attractive (financially) precisely because it is unattractive otherwise at a personal level.
- It is conservative and has relatively low innovation – which means it is ripe for breakthrough.
- Whilst you can't easily grow volume, you can grow value.

---

The relative attractiveness of growth opportunities in the funeral industry has not escaped the attention of new players. Even as long ago as 1994, changes were mooted in the industry in a feature on 'The New British Way of Death' appearing in *The Times* (20 November 1994), which is examined below.

## The 'supermarket of death' – the French way

Around 1990, Michel Leclerc (who was part of the Leclerc family famed for their French supermarket operation) opened his first 'Supermarché de Mort' in Paris. By 1994 he had 60 supermarket franchises, 200 smaller shops and one-third of the French funerals business. In 1995 he entered the UK.

Leclerc's growth concept was to 'apply the technology of the food supermarket to the funeral industry'. In place of black, the Roc Leclerc colour scheme was blue and yellow, and in place of dim bulbs and heavy velvet curtains was strip lighting and stripped-pine shelving. All the paraphernalia of death were on display, with a price tag. Mr Weller (the UK franchise manager) said, 'We aim to charge between 20 and 30 per cent less than elsewhere but, above all, to offer the widest possible range, which our customers can view without the pressure of having a funeral director at their shoulder.'

Sadly, this innovative growth strategy, whilst being ultra-successful in France, proved a failure in the UK. What appeared to have been missed by Leclerc here is that:

- the British attitude to death was very different culturally from that of the French, who were accustomed to a more open approach;

- Catford, a not-so-trendy place in south London, was probably not the best place to enter the market; and

- the entry strategy picked an unfavourable point in the economic cycle.

## Conclusions

What emerges, therefore, from the five competitive forces is a cosy industry structure ripe for innovation and restructuring, offering better quality at a much more acceptable price. Before we leave this example, there are a few more points which need to be made.

- When analysing the five competitive forces, you must try to put to the back of your mind which particular player you are. Otherwise, the analysis of the industry itself will become confused with your own particular position.

- You may need to do more than one analysis using the five forces, depending on whether you have in effect more than one market to analyse. For example, in the funerals business you would need to do a separate analysis for: the pre-need market; the funeral itself; the aftercare market; and a new, dot.com market.

To summarize, the main benefits of the five competitive forces are that they:

- are much more incisive in analysing competitor opportunities and (particularly) threats than the 'opportunities and threats' part of a SWOT analysis;

- can provide a prophetic view of industry changes (especially in margin levels) and in competitive structure and financial performance generally;

- can give you real insights into potential strategic options and into critical success factors;

- can provide more substance for scenario development; and

- help to prioritize the areas in which it is most/least important to grow.

## The industry mindset

Besides the five competitive forces, which influence the quality of growth within a market, we also see a sixth force – the 'industry mindset' (Grundy 1995). This can be defined as: 'The expectations and assumptions about the competitive rules of the game and the levels of financial returns in an industry.'

The industry mindset plays a major role in shaping industry change (as in the funerals business), thus transforming Porter's five competitive forces model from a static into a much more dynamic model. Figure 2.11 adapts Porter's forces by showing how these five forces interrelate with each other and also how the industry mindset is at the very hub of competitive pressure. It does this by:

- positioning the industry mindset as the central, sixth force, which plays a profound role in shaping the other five competitive forces; and

- explaining how the other five forces interact with one another.

To illustrate the final point, buyer power is closely linked to substitutes (via companies deciding to 'do-it-themselves') and also to supplier power (via demand/supply imbalance). Also, entrants may restructure the industry,

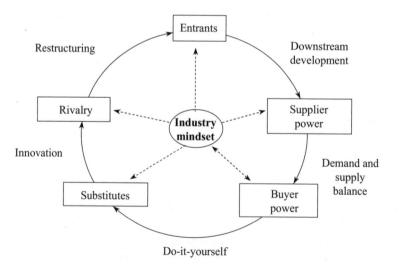

**Fig. 2.11**   Porter's five forces and the industry mindset.

impacting on competitive rivalry. Or suppliers themselves might enter the industry via downstream development.

Finally, substitutes and rivalry might together provoke fresh industry innovation. Few players with a longer-term stake in the industry will sit idly by and watch their market position significantly eroded by new sources of competition.

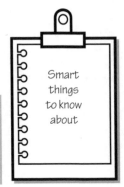

---

THE INDUSTRY MINDSET

- You don't need to take anything in the industry as 'given'.
- You *can* change the rules of the game.
- You *should* change the rules of the game.

---

The industry mindset can play a profound influence over market dynamics. The prevailing industry mindset may send signals to players adjacent to the market, attracting new entrants because of prevailing growth and profit expectations. For instance, going back to the funerals example, the cosy environment has now attracted new entrants, who have entered by acquisition.

The industry mindset may also have an impact on the role of buyer power and on substitutes. This impact can occur by influencing buying criteria and also the switching criteria of buyers. Buyers may have narrow perceptions about what substitutes are available and may also have inaccurate expectations about how new substitutes will perform (for example, they may never even think of planning their own funeral). They may also make assumptions, for instance that their purchase will not result in rapid obsolescence.

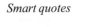

*Smart quotes*

'Companies that create the future do more than satisfy customers, they constantly amaze them.'

Hamel & Prahalad

'The biggest constraint is almost inevitably the external mindset, the culture of the organization, especially of the top people. They don't tend to see new opportunities in the same way as younger people further down the organization can see them. So the lenses through which they see external change are biased, basically, in favour of what they are currently doing.'

Murray Steele, Cranfield School of Management (2000)

## Customer life-cycles and the buying experience

In the mobile telephone market in the 1990s, first-time customers initially had poorly-defined buying criteria. They had even less well-defined switching criteria. Having made their first mobile telephone purchase, within a matter of months they learnt of the full cost burdens, the limitations of the hardware and of the particular network it is reliant on. Perhaps within months (or even weeks), the customer might become aware that substitute networks (as well as substitute handsets themselves) exist. In a relatively short period, the buyers' switching criteria are likely to crystallize, based on their learning about the opportunities and often severe limitations of the product.

SMART VOICES

A NOT-SO-SMART QUOTE

On Tesco's thinking of going into financial services (in the late 1990s) and mortgages:

'But that's not fair!'

Senior manager of a leading UK building society

*Exercise – an imaginary funeral business start-up*

Now imagine that you are 45 and have just been liberated (the new word for 'made redundant') from a senior director's role in a major corporation. You have received a pay-off of £200,000. You do not wish to go back into another high-flying, big, corporate job, as it is simply too stressful, perhaps leading to an early death. So, you hit on the wonderful idea of starting up a funeral business. How would you enter the market?

If the above were set as an examination question, it would be very tempting (and most managers would be tempted) to race into the 'what' and the 'how' of the start-up. But this is not really the most effective approach (although it might be efficient in the short-term). Instead, a superior approach might be to establish some lines of enquiry. Some useful ideas would be as follows.

- Work backwards from customer need – what do they want but are not getting, and what is being delivered badly or inefficiently?

- Which customers do you wish to target? Here, the segmentation is quite complex – for example you can distinguish between:
  - unpredictable versus predictable deaths (e.g. terminal illnesses);
  - different age ranges;
  - different income and wealth levels;
  - multicultural variations;
  - religious, agnostic and atheist customers (the latter two categories being substantial); and
  - pre-need versus after-the-event (i.e. after the death) customers.

- What needs are you going to meet? For instance:
  - mourning;
  - remembrance; and
  - (possibly) celebration – why does it have to be so depressing?

- What psychological and economic value might a customer place on a wonderful funeral – and how could you price this?

- Which activities will deliver value, and how might you do these differently?
  - the funeral itself;
  - body collection, storage, and disposal;
  - body presentation and preservation (embalming and cryogenics);
  - catering (for the living);
  - grief counselling (both after and – in terminal cases – before death); and/or
  - wills (for everyone – as death is a certainty).

- How?
  - insourcing of activities (see above);
  - outsourcing of activities; and/or
  - joint ventures.

- What are the possible distribution channels?
  - a retail network;
  - telephone call-centre (but one which is pleasant and does not keep you waiting!);
  - the Internet; and/or
  - a sales force or agents.

GROWTH DRIVERS

1  Growth possibilities need to be understood, through using external and internal growth drivers.
2  The quality of growth is largely determined by the five competitive forces.
3  Apparently very 'attractive' industries are often not so attractive precisely because of their *perceived* attractiveness (i.e. through competitive rivalry), and notably so in the example of the funeral industry.
4  The five competitive forces do change over time, as the industry life cycle unfolds.
5  The mindset of the industry is a force equally important to the forces of buyer power, supplier power, entry barriers, substitutes and rivalry.
6  'Uncertainty' is not just a black box, but can be analysed, using scenarios and the uncertainty grids.
7  Industry structure is not a 'given' – it can be challenged by cunning, and through innovative thinking.

Smart
things
to know
about

# 3

# Diagnosis of Growth Issues

## *Introduction*

In this chapter we look at how growth constraints should be diagnosed through 'fishbone' analysis. We then consider how growth opportunities can be made more visionary through 'wishbone' analysis. This also helps us to understand all the factors which may need to line up to make it a success.

To illustrate wishbone analysis, we use the Dyson Appliances case study, which also illustrates how the industry mindset can be challenged. The Dyson case illustrates the imperative of thinking through the sustainability of the growth drivers, favourable competitive forces and competitive advantage, into new phases of growth. The 'attractiveness/implementation-difficulty' (AID) grid is then introduced to help in prioritizing which areas of the growth problem or opportunity should be addressed.

## Fishbone analysis

Fishbone analysis is a very quick and easy way of going behind the more immediate definition of a growth problem or opportunity. For instance, Fig. 3.1 illustrates why growth strategy is frequently not well implemented. This can be due to a variety of reasons or underlying root causes. These include, for example, having too abstract a strategic vision, not fully thinking through implementation, or through having too many unprioritized activities.

There are some important guidelines for using fishbone analysis. First, the 'dos'.

• First, identify the symptom of the cause and position it over towards the right-hand side. Where there are a number of possible symptoms, you might need to analyse several problems (and thus draw up several fishbones). Or you may need to summarize a number of issues into a single, overarching fishbone.

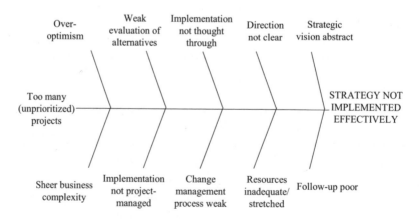

**Fig. 3.1**  Fishbone analysis.

- Then make sure that the root causes are the *real* root causes (or at least quite close to being root causes). If you can still ask the question 'why?', then you are still operating at the level of symptoms, not causes.

- Use your common sense to understand at what point you should cease going back up the causal chain. Thus 'lack of leadership skills' for most purposes is a satisfactory root cause of sluggish growth, rather than going back to 'the Board appointed the wrong leader' or 'there were no really suitable candidates'. (You do not need to go back to the dawn of time to necessarily scope and diagnose a problem.)

And the 'don'ts'.

- Don't worry about whether the fishbone causes should go vertically or downwards – there is no special priority in where they are positioned; they are all equivalent. Most fishbones are more complete if they are drawn up in a creative flow, rather than in some pre-structured manner. If you do want to prioritize the fishbones, write the root causes on self-adhesive notes and then move then around, perhaps in order of difficulty, or degree of influence, or perhaps their attractiveness.

- Don't clutter up the analysis with sub-bones off a main fishbone on the very same sheet of paper. This produces a visually complex, messy and hard-to-interpret picture. Where appropriate, do a mini-fishbone analysis for a particular cause or sub-bone on a separate page.

- Don't forget to consider the external causes as well as the internal root causes, and also the tangible versus the less-tangible causes of the original symptom.

Some generic systems that appear to be at work across many fishbone analyses are:

- the competitive environment;

- operations (internal);

- the wider environment;

- the customer;

- resource availability;

- decision making;

- politics;

- culture and style;

- structure and skills; and

- financial imperatives and pressures.

Figure 3.2 plots the main interdependencies of these systems. By creating a variety of fishbones for quite different issues, it is quite usual to find a small number of themes coming up over and over again. Often these are inter-related. We suggest that you use this picture to stimulate thinking about the possible root causes, or as a quick check on their completeness.

## Growth constraints and fishbone analysis

Even where it is entirely appropriate to tackle a big growth challenge head-on, it is still worthwhile breaking it down into specific breakthrough projects. For example, in the mid-1990s Tesco was simultaneously hit by

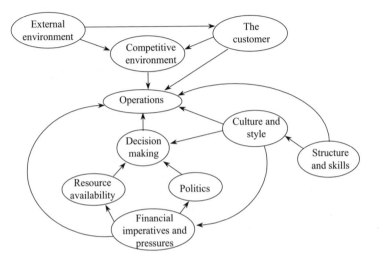

**Fig. 3.2** Generic systems in fishbone analysis.

the effects of prolonged recession, government restrictions on new out-of-town supermarket expansion, and a price war triggered by new entrants.

Out of a number of breakthrough areas, one in particular – culture – was chosen for a new focus. Here, culture was seen to be a potential impediment to future growth. Initially it was unclear as to how to tackle this and what was likely to come out of it. This breakthrough went through a process of transformation into practical projects to put the infrastructure in place for a superior growth-rate, which would in time improve culture. These included the following.

- Tesco superior customer services, through the 'one-in-front' policy (if there was a queue of more than one customer, further checkouts would be opened where possible).

- Service training for front-line store staff.

- Investment in management training (often with a behavioural focus).

- Simplification of processes at head office (making the retail head office interface easier to deal with, thereby reducing the sense of there being 'two cultures').

### Case study – strategic amnesia at a major computing company

A few years ago, a consultant was asked to facilitate a series of key account strategies at a major computer company. One part of the account had fallen badly behind budget and the fishbone was looking more depressing by the second. In a state of inspiration, the facilitator ripped off the flipchart, throwing it to the side of the room, saying:

*'This is so bad I am going to give you strategic amnesia: if you were to forget being in this key account and be looking to enter it from scratch, what would you want to achieve, and how would you achieve that through a re-entry strategy?'*

At a practical level, the key benefits of fishbone analysis are that it:

- helps diagnose a problem in much greater depth, helping to scope strategic issues much more effectively;

- reduces the tendency for managers to talk about the same issues over and over again – just using different words creates greater confusion and slows progress significantly; and

- communicates the scope and the key reasons for the problem in a politically neutral way – it is an essential technique for managing upwards.

Q: When should you use fishbone analysis?

A: There are several reasons:

- to understand past growth failures;
- to understand current growth constraints; and
- to anticipate future growth problems – and to head them off.

Smart answers to tough questions

## Growth opportunities and wishbone analysis

Whilst fishbone analysis is a very successful technique for diagnosing current or past growth problems, it does not deal readily with opportunity. To tackle growth opportunities, we use 'wishbone' analysis. Wishbone analysis is depicted (see Fig. 3.3) as the opposite of fishbone analysis. This is to present us moving into the future, rather than working backwards into past causes.

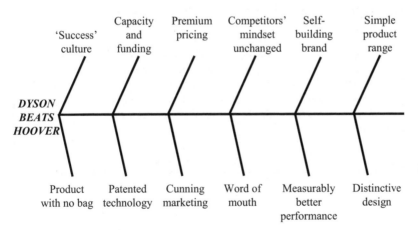

**Fig. 3.3**  Wishbone analysis.

At the start of the wishbone is its vision for growth (or in Spice Girls strategy terms, what we really, really want). It is important to make this vision for growth stretching and specific, otherwise we will not get our minds around what needs to be aligned to achieve this.

SMART ANSWERS TO TOUGH QUESTIONS

Q: What is wishbone analysis?

A: It is what needs to line up to give you what you really, really want.

The bones of the wishbone represent the alignment factors which are both necessary and sufficient to achieve this vision for growth. As we will see in the next section, which includes the Dyson case study, these alignment factors can be prioritized using the importance–uncertainty grid.

In order to complete the link to implementation, it is often useful to take the wishbone analysis a level deeper. This can be done by developing mini-wishbones, which will provide the necessary and sufficient conditions for a particular bone of the wishbone.

Having introduced wishbone analysis, let us now illustrate it with the Dyson case study.

*Smart quotes*

'If you cannot remember a mission statement (I cannot remember our old one), if you have to refer to something, that's wrong. To me, any mission statement which "we will have care for our customers, be nice to our staff, be nice to grey squirrels on Sundays", you know, you have gone to sleep.'

Lord Thurso, MD of Champneys Health Resort

'Every single one of them seemed to miss the point: that here was an innovation of real benefit to the customer, a massive leap from a crappy old carpet-sucker to a cleaner of total efficiency and undiminishable power. For each manufacturer in turn, it represented an opportunity to bring out a new product with a major technical advantage over their competitors. The most ironic in this respect was Goblin, who had trouble finding time to see me because they had all their staff on a two-day week because sales were so low.'

James Dyson, *Against the Odds*

## Case study – Dyson Appliances

**From inventor to entrepreneur**
Dyson's breakthrough in the carpet-cleaning appliances business demonstrates the importance of aligning all critical areas of the business, both internally and externally, in order to deliver value-based, sustainable growth.

In the mid-1990s, James Dyson, founding chairman of Dyson Appliances, decided to take on other players in the domestic carpet-cleaning appliances industry with a rather different proposition. He decided to discard the taken-for-granted assumption that such devices needed a bag. Dyson decided that, far from adding value for the customer, the bag was actually an unnecessary cost and a bother to replace. Worse, Dyson contended that the bag itself actually reduced the effective power, and thus the performance, of the carpet-cleaner. Dyson's new product, a distinctively designed, yellow, expensive and bagless floor-cleaner, gained leadership in the UK carpet-cleaning market.

James Dyson invented and patented a device which enabled his cleaners to do without a bag, using a very fast circling vortex of air. The dust was drawn up into a Perspex tube or cylinder, where it was then dropped. Periodically, the user would empty out this cylinder without producing a small dust storm.

**Going for competitive knockout**

Now Dyson could have stopped at this point in designing his strategy, but he decided not to do so. Instead, he set about achieving a compelling customer-pull, and a dominant competitive advantage. Intuitively, James Dyson recognized that to leapfrog over companies like Hoover and Electrolux, he needed to align a number of points of competitive leverage. Only then could he secure a financial advantage. Each one of the points of competitive leverage procures financial value.

So let us now represent these points of leverage using wishbone analysis. The wishbone analysis in Fig. 3.3 highlights just how many points of competitive leverage Dyson focused on. It also emphasizes how dependent his strategic success was on areas where he had relatively low influence (for example, on the assumption that the major industry competitors would not change their mindset significantly). Figure 3.3 also emphasizes how Dyson did not just set about exploiting its strategy from a technology-led point of view. In particular, he experimented with marketing innovation to achieve a compelling advantage. For instance, he offered his products at half-price to electrical goods retail salespeople to encourage trial. Figure 3.3 in its totality shows how well Dyson's strategic thinking and his strategic vision were articulated.

*Smart quotes*

'Strategic thinking is almost like a "Road to Damascus" experience, where suddenly you see a "Wooh!" and it becomes clear, and everything changes. So it is the start of clarity.'

Phil Davies, Cranfield School of Management

The results of this strategy were spectacular. In a short time, Dyson had achieved a major share of the market. In two and a half years, Dyson had moved from employing fewer than 20 people to employing 300, and in the year 2000, the number of employees stood at 1500.

According to *The Times* (8 February 1997), Dyson had reached a turnover of more than £100mn per annum in the three years since the launch of its core product, enabling him to buy a £3mn country house as his new home. Margins were rumoured to be of the order of those of the Body Shop in its heyday. His book, *Against the Odds*, is a fascinating account of this success.

### Creating 'built-in success'

When a growth strategy is targeted at achieving real dominance, it is perhaps rare to find that this is achieved through getting only a small number of factors right. It usually involves getting a considerable number of things right, and having favourable circumstances and good timing.

Where strategic success proves elusive, this may well be where just one, two or possibly three factors were not aligned completely. Dyson's success was achieved by working backwards from customer value and by engineering his entire activities to deliver that value. Some of these factors may be to do with the *competitive* strategy, some due to its implementation. James Dyson's own capability is the 'backbone' of the wishbone, being critical to implementation.

The various bones on the wishbone are interdependent. When they co-exist, additional value is created. For instance, the bottom bones of the wishbone deliver a natural and impelling demand for the product. The top bones help to lower its costs, increase its price, protect that price and facilitate expansion. By taking wishbone analysis as a whole, the various factors will differ both in their degree of *importance* and in terms of *influence* levels. This leads to a more in-depth analysis, to extend the domain of our control over the strategic vision, helping identify (and reduce) the likely implementation gap. Another cut to the analysis is how uncertain these factors are.

In Dyson's case, the assumption that 'competitors' mindset is likely to remain unchanged' appeared to be both very important and something over which Dyson had low influence. Had Dyson's competitors been able to counteract directly, this might easily have destroyed value through much-reduced volumes, reduced prices, increased discounting and also by pushing up operating costs. Therefore, a critical issue for Dyson was *how* did he encourage them to believe that by continuing to sell machines with a separate bag this offered the best route forward? Obviously, the fact that he had a strong patent protection was a useful tactic. But by encouraging a public debate on the relative merits of 'bag' versus 'no bag', he encouraged them to dig into (and become more committed to) their existing mindset.

*Smart quotes*

'Hamilton Beach, for example, said, "You've got two minutes to convince us" ... Why was it I who had to convince them? ... If the product were good, why should they need convincing? I knew they were loonies anyway, because they wouldn't let me use the word "suck". Presumably because it hinted at fellatio, which would have been unseemly, or because if something "sucks" in American slang, then it is bad. These people were nuts.'

James Dyson, *Against the Odds*

If we now stand back to look at the evolution of Dyson's wishbone, a review of his growth strategy might well now be advisable, especially as Dyson faces a number of transitions. In Dyson's growth strategy, for example, key uncertainties lie in the following areas.

- Patents – which expire.

- Cunning marketing has been imitated by Electrolux.

- The word-of-mouth effect may no longer be as strong, the Dyson product being in part fashion-dependent and not quite as novel at the present time.

- Customers sometimes queried its 'measurably better performance' – which is very hard to measure objectively.

- Its design style has been imitated by, for example, competitors.

- Competitors' mindsets *did* change (for example, many competitors sell a single-cyclone model, although in a court case won by Dyson in late 2000, Hoover was asked to withdraw its lookalike 'Vortex' range).

- Premium pricing is now under some pressure from discounting.

In addition to these particular wishbone alignment factors, we will leave it to the reader to query whether other factors might by now be both important and becoming increasingly uncertain. Figure 3.4 can be used to position these assumptions. Also, the factors driving Dyson's external and internal growth are perhaps not now so favourable, unless new products or technologies are brought out that are equally attractive to customers.

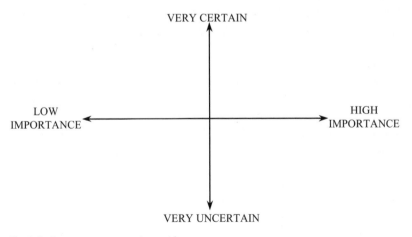

**Fig. 3.4** Importance–uncertainty grid.

So, whilst Dyson Appliances has had a most dramatic and successful growth strategy to date, clearly its competitive challenges are now mounting.

The above case on Dyson underlines the following.

- The ongoing need for strategic thinking – to sustain growth and to avoid complacency.

- Competitive advantage has to be continuously reinvented.

- The rewards from a quantum level of competitive advantage are quantifiable – and in economic terms.

- Two key strategic challenges are: (a) to know your customer better than they know themselves; and (b) to always be in a position to outguess and to pre-empt competitors in your search for reasonable growth.

### Dyson – case study postscript

By the late 1990s and the early 2000s Dyson Appliances faced increased challenges, particularly in the following ways.

- Imitation – Hoover launched the single-cyclone bagless machine in the late 1990s, copied by Electrolux, Panasonic and others, diminishing Dyson's unique selling point.

- Customer learning – over the period 1996–2001, an increasing number of Dyson users become disenchanted about some respects of Dyson products (for example, the product's weight, its reliability, the cost of filters, the attachments falling off). Against the background of this perception, in early 2001 the *Daily Mail* ran a provocative campaign 'For and Against Dyson', which highlighted a number of similar problems experienced by the general market.

- Growth potential – it was quite likely that, by 2001, the UK market was reaching saturation point and prices might be about to drop (especially with European entrants coming into the UK). This might culminate in a price war.

- Organizational resources – now that Dyson has over 1500 employees, would the company retain its entrepreneurial feel or might it begin to suffer from some of the malaise which affects many other large and mature organizations?

## Prioritization – attractiveness/implementation-difficulty (AID) analysis

We now look at the relative attractiveness and its difficulty of implementation, and begin to evaluate growth strategies at a micro-level, from a number of perspectives:

- one can prioritize a portfolio of growth strategies, any one of which can be undertaken;

- mutually exclusive growth strategies can be prioritized;

- different options for implementing a particular growth strategy can be evaluated; or

- the different parts or activities within a growth-related activity can be prioritized.

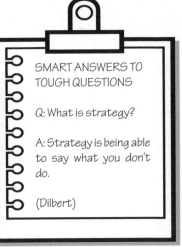

SMART ANSWERS TO TOUGH QUESTIONS

Q: What is strategy?

A: Strategy is being able to say what you don't do.

(Dilbert)

Sometimes parts of a possible growth strategy can be undertaken without doing others. For example, buying a business is a project, but the constituent parts of the business can be regarded as sub-projects to be retained or possibly disposed of. Even where a strategy does consist of a number of discretionary sub-parts, which are not themselves discretionary (such as a training strategy), it is still possible to display their individual positionings on an attractiveness/implementation-difficulty (AID) grid. Without doubt, some parts of the training will be more difficult than others to implement – and will thus have different horizontal positionings on the AID grid (see Fig. 3.5).

The AID grid enables trade-offs to be achieved between strategies. The vertical dimension of the picture focuses on benefits less costs. The horizontal dimension represents the total difficulty over time to implement the growth strategy. This time is the time up until delivery of results, and not of completion of earlier project phases. This tool enables a portfolio of possible growth projects to be prioritized. Figure 3.6 illustrates a hypothetical case.

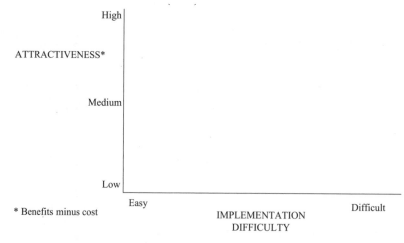

**Fig. 3.5**   AID analysis.

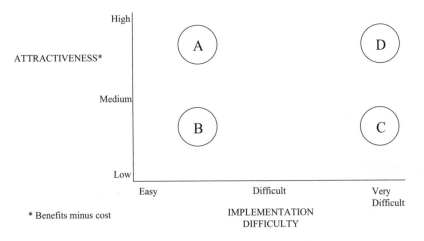

High

ATTRACTIVENESS*

Medium

Low

A          D

B          C

Easy            Difficult            Very
                                     Difficult

* Benefits minus cost          IMPLEMENTATION
                               DIFFICULTY

**Fig. 3.6**   AID analysis – example.

Growth strategy A is seen as being both very attractive and relatively easy to implement. This project is non-contentious and will probably be given the go-ahead. Growth strategy C is relatively difficult – it will probably end up being zapped unless it can be reformulated to make it both a lot more attractive and easier.

Growth strategy D presents the biggest dilemma of all. Although it appears to be very attractive, it is also very difficult to implement. Yet managers will tend to focus on the attractiveness of the project rather than its actual difficulty. When using the AID tool at Hewlett-Packard, this happened twice. Quite separately, two 'D-type' strategies were identified and as managers spent more time analysing them, commitment to action levels built up.

Strategies in the north-east zone do present us with some interesting management dilemmas. Following up one HP school of thought, one viewpoint is that it is unlikely to be worthwhile doing these projects, because realistically the organization will lack the commitment to drive them through.

However, a second HP school of thought is that such growth projects merely represent a challenge for creative thinking – as long as they are potentially very attractive, it may be very fruitful to do this.

Initially, one wondered whether this was perhaps an example of management heroism, but on reflection this philosophy fitted in well with the notion of 'breakthrough management', or *hoshin*. Indeed, if one were to seek out the easiest of growth opportunities, then no doubt these will also be easy for our competitors, thus not giving us a sustainable advantage.

A particularly cunning plan is to target growth projects which, whilst they are likely to be between 'very difficult' and 'Mission Impossible' for others to implement, we will find them easier. Here, Mission Impossible (or 'MI') is just off the page, to the east of the AID grid.

If we do decide to target projects, which are very difficult, then following the *hoshin* philosophy, it is important to narrow the focus to a very small number of projects within a specific period of time. It is very unlikely that more than three can be undertaken simultaneously without distraction of organizational attention and loss of energy generally.

The positionings on the AID grid are likely to be relatively tentative unless tested out using other techniques. For example:

- the 'attractiveness' of the project may require further analysis using value driver and cost driver analysis – see Chapter 8 – ultimately, this attractiveness can be financially quantified, albeit perhaps approximately;

- the implementation difficulty can be tested out using forcefield analysis and stakeholder analysis – see later in this chapter; and

- the difficulty over time can be visualized using the difficulty-over-time curve – see Fig. 7.5 on p. 225.

A useful rule of thumb for the less experienced user of the AID grid, or for those who have not used forcefield and stakeholder analysis to check out their horizontal positioning, is that:

- if you think the project is easy, it is probably difficult;

- if you think the project is difficult, it is probably very difficult;

- if you think the project is very difficult, it is probably MI.

One manufacturing company invented a fifth category, which is even worse than MI, but because its letters are identical to a well-known UK furniture retailer and have other negative, albeit humorous, connotations, we will leave this to your imagination.

To summarize, AID analysis can be used:

- to prioritize strategic breakthroughs as a portfolio;

- to evaluate business plans;

- to evaluate the sub-components of a strategic breakthrough or project; and

- to track (in real time) an area of strategy implementation.

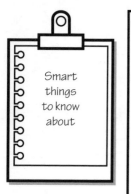

DIAGNOSIS OF GROWTH ISSUES

1 Fishbone analysis helps to diagnose past and present growth blockages and constraints.
2 It can also be used to anticipate future constraints.
3 Wishbone analysis helps define what needs to line up to give you 'what you really, really want'.
4 The alignment factors need to be sustainable – the wishbone needs to be reinvented periodically to maintain growth.
5 Competitive imitation can throw the wishbone off balance (as it threatened to do at Dyson).
6 Growth issues and actions need to be carefully prioritized using the AID grid.

Its key benefits are that it:

• is a quick and easy technique to use; and

• is a visual way of representing and debating priorities.

# 4

# Cunning Options for Growth

## Introduction

Specific breakthroughs are an important focus for the growing organization. In this chapter we explain what these growth breakthroughs are and how we can arrive at them – using a number of lines of enquiry. We then look specifically at options using the 'octopus' grid to generate them, and the strategic option grid and the General Electric grid to evaluate and prioritize them.

Finally, we look at the range of options which BMW had at the time it acquired Rover Group, demonstrating the power of the strategic option grid. Might BMW have done something different from buying Rover had they used the strategic option grid, we wonder?

'Be extremely subtle, even to the point of formlessness. Be extremely mysterious, even to the point of soundlessness. Thereby you can be the director of the opponent's fate.'

Sun Tzu, *The Art of War*

## Growth breakthroughs – the hoshin philosophy

Once we have done an initial issues analysis – based, perhaps, on a gap analysis – we might now begin to scope the potential for strategic break-throughs in the business. Here, a 'strategic breakthrough' is defined as: a specific programme of strategic action which will produce a step-change in the company's competitive position, its financial performance and/or in its capability.

The idea of 'breakthrough' comes originally from the Japanese philosophy of *hoshin*. This simple philosophy states that any organization can only realistically accomplish between one and three strategic breakthroughs within a specific time period (for instance, 18 months to two years).

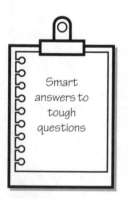

*Smart answers to tough questions*

Q: Why do *hoshin* growth breakthroughs need to be so few in number?

A: Because:

- organizations cannot hold attention on many breakthroughs simultaneously;
- this helps to concentrate internal resources;
- it increases speed and momentum of action – as there are fewer distractions; and
- competitors do not usually manage this way – making them more vulnerable.

There are several reasons why an organization can only implement such a small number of growth breakthroughs, including:

- the need to concentrate resources to achieve a critical mass;

- to enable strategies to be easily communicated;

- to mobilize sufficient intent and power within the organization; and

- to help managers to understand what is really, really important.

One of the reasons why the law of breakthrough analysis is of such small numbers (one to three at any one time) is because of the organization's cognitive limitations. In cognitive psychology it has been said that:

*'The average person can hold up to five things in their head at any one time, whilst a genius can hold seven things in their head at one time. But a below-average person can hold just three things in their head at any one time.'*

Hence the rule of cognitive psychology of 'five, plus or minus two'. As we saw in Chapter 1, it is very difficult to simultaneously pursue more than three breakthroughs that impact across the organization.

The techniques in Chapters 2 and 3 provide the necessary, but not the sufficient, conditions for evolving a breakthrough growth strategy. In addition, you will need to become creative in your strategic thinking – which involves a major element of imagination and play. This may not come naturally to you or to your team, who probably spend the vast majority of their time on tactical management.

*Smart quotes*

'What happened on Thursday night was that our thinking became much more pinpointed on areas where we could make some extra value, to outstrip the market in some sort of way … The focus on two or three areas was the breakthrough on Thursday night.'

Jo Ranger, ZIFA Life

The creative process entails a good deal more than merely brainstorming. Brainstorming, whilst laudable as a means of generating ideas, typically produces a mass of disconnected, disjointed and largely unrelated ideas. This mass of ideas can actually cause more problems than it may solve. This is particularly true of unstructured brainstorming.

The creative process is best harnessed instead by using some thought triggers to develop strategic lines of enquiry, almost along the lines of detective work – or the 'Lieutenant Columbo approach'. Some of these lines of enquiry might require expansion, development or playful experimentation in combination with other creative thoughts. Creative thinking does have to be targeted, at least to an extent, otherwise it can go off in an inappropriate or unhelpful direction.

Figure 4.1 maps out a more (semi-)structured creative process than mere brainstorming. This figure shows a non-linear process, a veritable cycle of creativity. This begins with our creating the right quality of thinking space to encourage creativity. This 'thought space' is needed for these two key reasons: to step out of everyday concerns and thought habits; and to allow for time and attention to develop the ideas more fully.

Next, we need to *stretch* our mindsets to embrace the possible – rather than getting ourselves bogged down in everyday clutter and in the detail of where we are now. This necessitates the need to search for both likely and less likely growth options. This process of search will then require a further phase of identifying the synergies between the key ideas which we have come up with. The next step is to go through the process of synthesizing the ideas to bring out the best combination. Finally, we need to think about creative ways in which we might build support for the idea's go-ahead, and for its implementation.

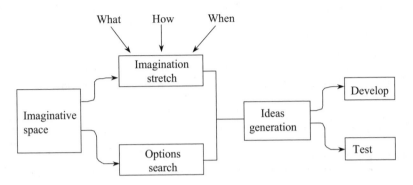

**Fig. 4.1** Creating strategic options.

In our next section we describe some recipes for creating lines of strategic enquiry. We then turn to the evaluation of strategic choices and further refinement of these ideas using the strategic option grid, where we also explore the impact of decision-making styles on strategic thinking. Finally, we apply the strategic option grid to the case of BMW/Rover.

## Lines of enquiry – the 'Columbo' approach

All of the techniques contained in this book contain at least some element of creativity – for example, when we are using the GE (General Electric) grid to understand the present position of a business, this can also be used to think about how a business unit might be radically repositioned. Visual approaches like the GE grid (which we see later on in this chapter) usually do enhance creativity. But in addition to these more visual approaches, it is also possible to use some less formal stimuli for generating creativity. These are best laid out in the following recipes for being creative. They consist of:

- creating lines of strategic enquiry;

'Kids are naive. They don't know what's possible and what's impossible. So they ask innocent questions ("Why can't you touch the stars?") and hope for impossible things ("Why can't learning be fun?"). Adults are smart. They know what's possible and impossible. So they don't ask silly questions and they don't hope for impossible things … The most precipitous fall in quizzicality takes place just after kids start school. But occasionally a dumb question lifts the blinds of orthodoxy just long enough to let in a ray of light from the future.'

Hamel & Prahalad

- challenging the constraints;

- working backwards from customers;

- beating your competitors;

- challenging the industry rules; and

- creating greater degrees of freedom – in the organization.

## Creating lines of enquiry

The recipes below are mainly concerned with generating sufficient vision and detachment from the detail. These recipes give you general suggestions for becoming more creative.

**Work backwards from the result, not from where you are now**
It is always a good idea to start by thinking about what you actually want to achieve in your growth strategy, rather than just by throwing up a good idea.

**Imagine the future – and how you succeeded in it**
Instead of beginning in the present, try the thought experiment of being in the future. It is frequently much easier to work back from the future rather than forwards from where you are now.

**Look at existing practices as if you were an alien visitor**
Most industries can be revolutionized by simply seeing their practices as 'strange', as if you were an alien. For instance, one major bank in Ireland actually instituted 'alien away-days' to look at its markets from scratch. This enabled it to fundamentally question its existing marketing strategy, shifting it towards a greater focus on human need as opposed to packaged products.

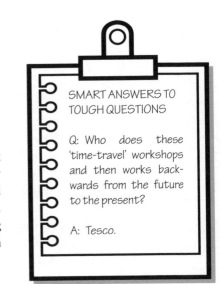

SMART ANSWERS TO
TOUGH QUESTIONS

Q: Who does these 'time-travel' workshops and then works backwards from the future to the present?

A: Tesco.

SMART ANSWERS TO TOUGH QUESTIONS

Q: How do you get to run an 'alien away-day'?

A: Get a management consultant to come in and be an alien, and to say they were just pretending to be a management consultant (not a difficult thing to do).

Smart
answers to
tough
questions

**Frequently go back to what you really, really want (the 'Spice Girls' strategy)**
The problem with much conventional strategic analysis is that analysing where you are now can root your mindset in your current position rather than in possibilities and potential. The Spice Girls song about going for what you really, really want reminds you to go back to your stretching goals. This is especially useful in a difficult situation and one which is emotionally or politically sensitive.

**Practice 'helicopter' thinking – avoid getting bogged down in detail**

A similar recipe is to remember to think as if you are looking down from a helicopter. This perspective can jolt you into a bigger appreciation of the context of an issue, and of the possibilities which it affords.

**If you were to invest more resources, would this give disproportionate value through growth?**

One approach is to relax the resource-based constraints associated with your current strategy. This may lead to a strategy with a bigger scope and one that exhibits greater economies of scale and dominance.

**Zero-base your strategy**

Alternatively, one might take away (mentally) all of the currently committed resource, and then reassemble new and perhaps different resources according to a new 'cunning plan'.

**Start from a very low resource-base and build up**

Linked to the above, a slightly more relaxed approach is to start again from a low base of resources and then increase them.

**Simplify the process**

Whilst processes may be seen as the area of operational management, often by doing something differently and more simply, you can transform a strategy. Not only might this reduce cost and be faster, but it might also add more customer value – complexity can often get in the way of realizing value.

*Challenging the constraints*

Challenging the constraints on growth can lead to some fruitful lines of enquiry. These prompts help you to step outside your current frame of reference. Many of the resistances to strategic thinking are due to taken-for-granted constraints.

### Wherever there are constraints, get more (not less) excited (the 'Joy of Constraints')

Whilst it is probably too late to write the equivalent (in strategy) of the famous book *The Joy of Sex*, a useful substitute would perhaps be *The Joy of Constraints*. In other words, if someone says 'We can't do that', then instead of just accepting that, try to think of a way around it, especially with the cunning plan.

### If there is a constraint, think why it is there and how it can be avoided

More specifically, it may help (rather than by resorting to simplistic brainstorming) to consider why a constraint exists in the future. Fishbone analysis (see Chapter 3) can help you here. In the same breath, by determining why it is there you are probably halfway to avoiding it.

### Focus on constraints one at a time, always beginning with the most critical one

This is a prescription from Goal Theory (Goldratt, 1990). Instead of staring at each constraint simultaneously, it is necessary to pick them out one at a time, to challenge and dissolve, usually beginning with the hardest. If that one is simply too daunting, pick off a number of the easier ones first.

### Working backwards from customers

Customers are potentially a fantastic source of inspiration for growth strat-

'Having watched her father snap a photograph, Dr Edward Land's three-year-old daughter asked if she could see the results *right now*. This innocent question set Land off on a quest to create instant photography. Years later, at Polaroid, Land reflected that "we really don't invent new products … the best ones are already here, only invisible, just waiting to be discovered".'

Hamel & Prahalad

egies – and one which is frequently ignored because it is felt to be embarrassing to ask customers what they think you could or should do.

Customers are a wonderful source of strategic thinking. It has been said that they are your unpaid strategy consultants.

**Have the 'out-of-body experience' – do 'psychic market research'**
Before conducting extensive market research, why not think about what your customers are likely to come up with anyway, were you to do market research. If you are able to enter fully into this simulation, which we call the 'out-of-body experience', then often you can elicit customers' attitudes, needs and what they are (and are not) prepared to pay for, almost as well as in doing actual market research.

**Be your own customer (physically)**
In most markets you can actually be your own customer. This is easiest in retail, financial services, leisure, publishing and telecommunications. But even in the business-to-business market you can make an enquiry to your own company (or to a competitor) and live through at least the front end of the process. The main reason why companies do not use this approach seems to be down to fear. Fear that they might find out that they are not as good as the average.

'Yet another way in which competition for the future is different from competition for the present is the timeframe. Today, speed is of the essence. Product life cycles are getting shorter, development times are getting tighter, and customers expect almost instantaneous service.'

Hamel & Prahalad

### How can you add more value to your customer?

Following on from an out-of-body experience, now think about how you can add even more value to your customer. If you were them, what other needs do you have which either are not currently being supplied or are being supplied poorly? Are you delivering value throughout the customer's main phase of consumption? What experiences, both before and after that core phase, can you also service?

### How can you avoid destroying or diluting value?

Most writers focus on value added, but by simply avoiding the destruction of customer value, or even merely its dilution, this can in turn generate real competitive advantage. Imagine, for example, that you were running a management course in a British hotel, a facility with no builders banging away, no sudden intrusions of staff chinking coffee cups whilst you are in mid-sentence. This is, unfortunately, just a dream.

'When one conceives of a company as a portfolio of competencies, a whole new range of potential opportunities typically opens up. We use the term white spaces to refer to opportunities that reside between or around existing product-based business definitions.'

Hamel & Prahalad

### If you are creating lots of value, capture more of it

Interestingly, many companies create value but sometimes fail to fully capture it. This might be due to highly competitive market conditions, or it might be due to a lack of innovative positioning and pricing.

### When is most value created/least value created over time?

One specific approach is literally to draw a curve of value added (as perceived by the customer) over their experience of the product or service. This is particularly useful for exploring customer value associated with services. For example, if a supplier were delivering a major consulting project, when would value actually be realized?

### How can something be made more convenient to buy?

Simply taking away the difficulties of buying something can lead to increased sales. Alternatively, making it easier (mentally, emotionally and physically) for the customer to buy more can facilitate increases in sales volume.

### How can something be made absolutely irresistible to buy?

More stretching still, set yourself the mental goal of making your proposition so compelling that it actually becomes irresistible. This can often be achieved by skilful management of the buying experience – and its psychology – on top of an already highly attractive product and service base. The buying process is, after all, a mental rehearsal of what consumption will be like, in large respect, so how can you give a flavour of that experience? What is your bait?

### How can customers sell you on your behalf?

Getting your customers to sell you is a great way to leverage your network of intangible resources. In the consulting industry this is called having a 'fox'. The role of the fox is to go down the holes in the organization to tell you where the rabbit is – you do not need to know how to find it yourself.

The fox is not only willing and doesn't want to get paid, but is also very good at it. But you must delight the fox first.

**What cunning plans would build customer or channel lock-in, preferably without them knowing it?**
Perhaps this one has a slightly manipulative feel about it. But in many competitive markets you may need this tip. To achieve this, you do need to either identify the things which will really turn the customer or channel on, and then get them addicted to these, or it may be that you skilfully create switching costs which would make it unthinkable to change supplier.

**Get customers to think of the financial value of your differentiated product or service**
In marketing it is not always self-evident that you should think about how much financial value the customers actually see in your delivery. You can indeed ask them 'What is it actually worth to you?'

*Beating your competitors*

Competitors, too, can be a source of significant inspiration – not merely to copy them but (ideally) to become tangibly better than them. Your competitors are equally fertile territory for you to generate new strategic thoughts.

**Study your competitors – and then do things even better**
Competitive analysis is not done particularly well by many companies. Some do no formal competitor analysis at all. Doing competitor analysis is, however, only the first stage to asking the question: 'How can we do things even better – that is, either better than how they do it or better than how we do it now?'

**Learn from how things are done in other industries**

Other industries can be fertile grounds for creative thought. For instance, many years ago, the author helped the UK Post Office to think through how it could protect its cost centres by organizing a lunch with Securicor service managers, who were able to suggest not building bulletproof centres but put forward ways of deceiving criminals so that they did not actually know where the real cash was.

**Can you build barriers to imitation?**

Whilst all of us strive to create competitive advantage, it is not always so obviously important to protect against imitation. The best forms of protection are to build multiple levels of naturally reinforcing competitive advantage. Here, whilst in theory each layer *might* be imitated, imitating all the layers of competitive advantage would be very difficult indeed.

## Challenging the industry rules

Besides the 'alien approach', which we saw earlier, challenging the ways in which value is created and captured – and how resources are managed – typically provokes powerful lines of enquiry.

**How can you change the rules of the game?**

The rules of the game are not fixed – and you can change them. Imagine, for example, if you were starting an estate agency industry from scratch at the present time. Would you have expensive BMWs for your senior sales agents? Would you be clearer about who your agents are actually working for to improve integrity and confidence? (Estate agents frequently work for both seller and buyer – they are in reality 'double agents'.)

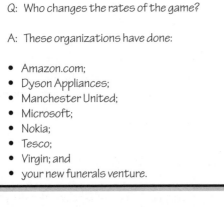

Q: Who changes the rates of the game?

A: These organizations have done:

- Amazon.com;
- Dyson Appliances;
- Manchester United;
- Microsoft;
- Nokia;
- Tesco;
- Virgin; and
- your new funerals venture.

Smart answers to tough questions

**If the rules of the game are changing in the future, how can you do this now?**

Rather than respond negatively or defensively to industry change, use scenario storytelling to see into the future. Then work out ways in which you can manifest that future yourselves – to beat competition.

**Abandon any existing mindset (at industry, company and personal levels)**

More systematically, begin by letting go of your existing mindset. This mindset can be multi-layered. Forget not only how the industry – and the company – currently does things, but also how you do things and even how you *think* about things.

**What would really put your competitors off-balance?**

Following on from earlier thinking on competitors, identify strategies for getting (and keeping) them off-balance. Temporary price reductions are unlikely to achieve this goal, but a series of well-phased products and/or service enhancements might.

**Where a competitor might find something difficult to do, how could you make it easy for you to do?**
True competitive advantage often does not come from anything superbly innovative but from doing something really, really well – something that comes to you naturally – but which a competitor is likely to find very difficult to implement. The proviso here, though, is that it must be strategically important!

## Creating greater degrees of freedom – in the organization

There are a number of ways of generating radical challenge within the organization – dealing with the art of the possible. Indeed, as we will now see, there are many ways of loosening up the organization to think more creatively about the strategies.

**Have a 'strategic amnesty'**
A powerful approach is to spend some time (even if just 20–30 minutes) with the team to talk about, and to let go of, past strategic failures. Usually there has never been the time or the safe opportunity to do this. By calling this a 'strategic amnesty', it is easier to flush things out and to let them go.

*Smart quotes*

'There are many characteristics that have made Jack Welch famous, notorious, feared, respected, and admired. One of Welch's least noted characteristics (and perhaps useful in a world marked by rapid shifts in customer priorities and rapid business-design obsolescence) is the absence of strong allegiance to the past. Welch has zero institutional memory. He has no loyalty to what went before. The phrase, "We've always done it this way" is meaningless to him.'

Hamel & Prahalad on Jack Welch – 'The CEO Without a Memory'

**Imagine you just started in the organization today**

This is a similar thought process to having strategic amnesia. Here, you forget your own experience, agendas and thought patterns which you have been socialized into by the organization. At the same time you can still access the knowledge you have gained from your experience – so you can have the best of both worlds. Besides being a fruitful line of enquiry for competitive strategy, this is also helpful in doing a strategic review (for yourself) of your own role.

**Remember Winnie the Pooh – always look for other options to how things are now done**

Remembering the plight of teddy in the *Winnie the Pooh* smart quote box, there may be a better way of doing things. This might be to do things differently or even to do quite different things to achieve your goals.

**Think about what natural turn-ons may exist (for customers or stakeholders) – what is the 'bait'?**

In Chapter 7, on implementation, we examine in greater depth the need to analyse stakeholders' (or customers') agendas. Here, we need to focus specifically on those things which will tempt commitment.

**Eliminate unnecessary turn-offs**

Here we focus on avoiding those things which may put off the key stakeholders (or customers).

*Smart quotes*

'Here is Edward Bear, coming downstairs now, bump, bump, bump, on the back of his head, behind Christopher Robin. It is, as far as he knows, the only way of coming downstairs, but sometimes he feels that there really is another way, if only he could stop bumping for a moment and think of it.'

A.A. Milne, *Winnie the Pooh*

**Where you have apparently low influence over something important, how can you get more influence?**

In any situation, our attention is likely to be drawn to those areas over which we have most apparent influence. It is less obvious that in fact we can often get further at a creative level by focusing instead on at least some areas over which we have little influence – and then trying to work out cunning plans for gaining more influence over them.

**Forget that anyone might be against your solution – deal with that later**
Stakeholders can sometimes be troublesome, and this can crowd-out your thought space, reducing opportunities to think differently. One tactic is to simply forget that they might be against you or even that they exist. Whilst influencing stakeholders is, of course, very, very important, this needs to be handled mentally quite separately.

**Create 'white space' – set aside exclusive time to focus solely on the problem**
A major perceived problem is frequently the sheer lack of time for strategic thinking. The result of this perception is that managers flit from problem to problem like super-bees, but rarely actually resolve any specific problem. Instead, you should focus on a single issue at a time. Also, you do need to allocate sufficient time that is completely clear of other concerns in order to address it. This can be done whilst travelling, in hotels or even in traffic jams.

**Do allow yourself to think out loud – even if an idea may seem silly to others**
This is a classic technique – which helps not just creativity but also to diffuse organizational politics. It should be prefaced perhaps by saying, 'I know this may be a stupid thought, but would you mind if I just think out loud?' This tactful approach gets people to listen and to be more open and sympathetic.

**If you can't think of a creative idea, who might?**
This prompt is absolutely not a last-ditch one. Indeed, you should always think about who might be able to get you to your goal of having strategic thoughts about a particular issue.

### Explain the problem to someone detached from it

A related approach is simply to talk through the problem with someone else. This is invariably helpful – and not merely to get direct input. The verbalizing of the problem in itself often generates strategic thinking.

### If you are stuck with a growth problem, leave the problem and go back to it later

Leaving a problem for a while may seem to be counter-intuitive when it is really bothering you. Paradoxically, however, this is frequently the best way of resolving it.

### If you have got a really good idea, how can you make it even better (and aim for 'total cunning')?

Here, we move from normal management through to 'cunning' and finally through to 'stunning' – that is, by being exceedingly clever and innovative.

### Ask your unconscious mind to look for a solution

An advanced approach is to ask your unconscious mind to work on it for you. With practice, this usually dissolves about half (or sometimes more) of the problem – and with a 90% reliability level.

### Imagine you are your own consultant, advising yourself

Here, it pays to conduct a special version of the 'out-of-body experience' – one of imagining you are your own management consultant. It is useful to couple this with, say, a thought experiment in which you are starting your first day in the organization, or in which you are re-entering the industry from scratch.

### Look first for a process of solving the problem, not necessarily for the solution

Einstein once said that the essence of genius was not to solve a problem but to understand the best process for solving it. In a Columbo-detective context, this is about working out recipes for generating fruitful lines of enquiry. For example, where we think about the possible motive for a murder, identifying all of those who might have known the victim, was there anything in the victim's life or recent activities that seemed dubious or out of character?

**Don't do brainstorming without a method of processing the ideas (especially screening)**
Relatively unstructured brainstorming is often not terribly valuable. Brainstorming, if indeed you are to do it, does need to be accompanied by some screening methodologies – for example, either the strategic option grid (see later on in this chapter) or the AID analysis (Chapter 7).

## *Generating options – the 'octopus' grid*

When generating growth options, there are two main approaches:

- to go direct to using the strategic option grid (see next section), having brainstormed some options, perhaps using the lines of enquiry in the last section; or

- alternatively, to use the semi-structured approach of the octopus grid.

The octopus grid focuses on eight major directions for growth. In Fig. 4.2, these are as follows.

- Geography – where to serve geographically.

- Market sectors – types of industry.

- Customer segments – different types of customer (within that industry).

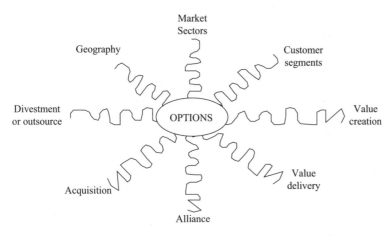

**Fig. 4.2** Octopus grid.

- Value creation – different aspects of customer need. For example, in the funerals business these might be: dealing with the body; dealing with the emotional issues, or with grief; having a family gathering; being remembered after death; and perhaps even celebrating the occasion.

- Value delivery – different ways of resourcing activities, or of distributing them to market (both order taking and order fulfilment).

- Alliance – finding a short- or longer-term partner(s) to collaborate with.

- Acquisition – buying another operation.

- Divestment or outsourcing – reconfiguring value; creating activities or business scope to produce more profitable operation and a sounder platform for future growth.

Again it might be helpful to begin with a 'zero-base' or 'alien' type of approach. For example, compare the following analysis in Table 4.1, which is for my own strategy consultancy, contrasting current and 'alien' strategies.

Table 4.1   Reinventing a management consulting business – the 'alien' approach.

|  | Current strategy | 'Alien' strategy |
| --- | --- | --- |
| Customer segments | Senior directors | CEO |
| Value creation | Learning how to do strategy and some strategic decisions | Board level strategy (only) |
| Value delivery | Personal contact | Personal contact and the Internet |
| Geography and base | UK and Europe – from UK barriers | US (base) and international scope |

The main interesting insight that came out of this analysis was that the consultant would probably be better running a business in the US, which is a larger market and more receptive to innovative thinking perhaps than Europe.

The key benefits of the Octopus grid are:

- it can be a quicker way of generating growth options than brainstorming; and

- it typically generates between 50% and 100% more options (in number).

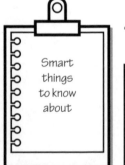

Smart things to know about

THE OCTOPUS GRID

- It can double the number of potentially viable options for you to customers.
- It helps you mix and match options more creatively.
- It can be the best way of generating the cunning plan.

## The strategic option grid – top-down

The criteria for choosing a growth strategy need to be predefined and explicit, rather than loose and unstructured. The strategic option grid (see Fig. 4.3) allows personal and strategic agendas to be thoroughly unscrambled.

| OPTIONS / CRITERIA | OPTION 1 | OPTION 2 | OPTION 3 | OPTION 4 |
|---|---|---|---|---|
| STRATEGIC ATTRACTIVENESS | | | | |
| FINANCIAL ATTRACTIVENESS* | | | | |
| IMPLEMENTATION DIFFICULTY | | | | |
| UNCERTAINTY AND RISK | | | | |
| ACCEPTABILITY (TO STAKEHOLDERS) | | | | |

* Benefits minus cost – net cashflow relative to investment

**Fig. 4.3**   Strategic option grid.

The row headings of the strategic option grid are generic criteria for appraising strategic options, and the column headings are strategic options (more than four columns can be used if necessary). Sometimes options are created by combining other options (and so, for example, option 3 could be a combination of options 1 and 2). Each option generates a different pattern of stakeholder influence, and thus of stakeholder acceptability. Each of the boxes on the strategic option grid can be scored high, moderate or low to indicate the option's overall attractiveness. (Note that the areas of uncertainty and risk and implementation difficulty have to be scored in reverse – that is, something that is 'highly difficult' is given a 'low attractiveness' score.)

Figure 4.4 shows an example of the use of the strategic option grid. It scores the telephone enquiry system of a railway that was to be privatized. Option 1 (closure) was strategically and financially attractive, but it was uncertain, difficult and less acceptable. Options 2 and 3 (cut costs and increase prices, respectively) looked marginally more attractive, but it was option 4 (obtain more centralized funding, raise prices and cut costs) which saved the organization.

| | Closure | Cost cutting | Price rises | Options 2 & 3 plus more funding |
| | 1 | 2 | 3 | 4 |
|---|---|---|---|---|
| Strategic attractiveness | ✱✱✱ | ✱ | ✱✱ | ✱✱✱ |
| Financial attractiveness | ✱✱ | ✱✱ | ✱✱✱ | ✱✱✱ |
| Implementation difficulty | ✱ | ✱✱ | ✱ | ✱✱ |
| Uncertainty and risk | ✱ | ✱✱ | ✱ | ✱✱ |
| Stakeholder acceptability | ✱ | ✱✱ | ✱ | ✱✱✱ |
| **Total score** | 8 | 9 | 8 | 13 |

Fig. 4.4 Strategic option grid – railway telephone enquiry system.

Before we look in more detail at the criteria (which can be tailored to your specific business or decision) it is important to stress that the strategic option grid is merely the starting point for thought. Even with what would appear to be a weak option, if we were to apply the creativity technique outlined earlier, we might well be able to craft a better option.

We now look at strategic choice criteria in more depth, and especially at the influence of stakeholders.

## Strategic attractiveness

Strategic attractiveness can be defined according to a number of factors including:

- market growth (present);

- market volatility;

- competitive intensity;

- future market growth;

- fit with own capability;

- fit to own brand;

- likely edge over competitors;

- scale of opportunity; and

- focus or possible dilution of own strategy.

In addition to the factors mentioned above, the GE grid described later on in this chapter, along with related analysis techniques, is a great help in going deeper into these criteria.

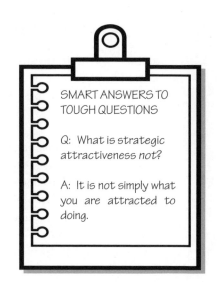

SMART ANSWERS TO TOUGH QUESTIONS

Q: What is strategic attractiveness *not*?

A: It is not simply what you are attracted to doing.

## Financial attractiveness

Financial attractiveness is based on the key value and cost drivers that underpin a strategic option. A value driver (which we explore further in Chapter 8) is defined as 'anything which directly or indirectly generates cash inflows, present and future, into the business' (Grundy, 1998). A cost driver is defined as 'anything which directly or indirectly generates cash outflows, present and future, out of the business'. Key criteria here could be:

- incremental sales volumes generated;

- premium pricing achieved;

- discounts avoided;

- costs reduced;

- costs avoided (for example by having one head office rather than two);

- accelerated or retarded strategy development; and

- share price impact.

## Implementation difficulty

Implementation difficulty needs to be anticipated *over the total time of implementation*, and not just during its early phase. Typical criteria of difficulty include the following:

- inherent complexity;

- clarity of implementation strategy;

- determination and commitment;

- resistances; and

- availability of resources and skills.

Implementation difficulty can also be assessed using the difficulty-over-time curve (see Chapter 7).

## Uncertainty and risk

Detailed factors for uncertainty and risk are diverse and are specific to the context of a particular option. However, some generic factors are:

- environmental uncertainty (will external conditions change?);

- management uncertainty (can we make it work?); and

- cultural uncertainty (will people adapt?).

The uncertainty grid (see Chapter 2) will help you to gain a more objective handle on these judgements.

## Stakeholder acceptability

Stakeholder capability will be explored in more depth in Chapter 7, so we will leave this until later.

*Applying the strategic option grid*

Standing back from the strategic option grid, there are a number of potential ways of using it. First, one can use it on a stand-alone basis to sort out high level options. These might be options for: (a) what to do, where these options are quite separate; (b) what to do, when there are a variety of routes to achieve the same goal; and (c) implementation options. Where options for 'different things we can do' are across the top of the grid, effectively the 'options for how to do it' are in a third dimension behind the page. All (ultimately) need exploring.

Secondly, the grid can be used before using the more detailed techniques contained in the rest of this book. Thirdly, the grid can be used *after* using the more detailed techniques (the GE grid, the uncertainty grids, etc.), and perhaps also after some selected data collection.

The advantage of *not* doing detailed analysis up-front is that more options can be thought through, and also this will minimize commitment to a course of action. (Typically, when data is collected, commitment to the course of action tends to increase.) The disadvantage of the more high-level approach is that in the wrong hands this might be subjective.

A number of caveats need to be observed in using the strategic option grid.

- In assessing strategic attractiveness, users will often rate highly simply because they are attracted to the opportunity or decision. In reality, however, the option may be unattractive due to its unfavourable market attractiveness, its likely competitive position, or both (and this weak position on the GE grid – see later on in this chapter).

- Financial attractiveness may be considered low simply because the decision requires longer-term investment. But provided that future returns are good, there are simple grounds for giving a more positive judgement.

- Implementation difficulty may be underestimated as only the early stage of implementation is thought through.

- Uncertainty and risk – again, key uncertainties may not be uncovered, resulting in a bias towards optimism. This requires further analysis using the importance–uncertainty grid (see Chapter 2).

- Stakeholder support – unless the positions of key stakeholders (now and in the future) have been thought through in detail, the view might be either under- or over-optimistic.

In summary, through formalization and visualization of the criteria for strategic choice of growth strategies, and in particular a formal stakeholder analysis, hopefully more informed choices can be made.

Once you have identified some interesting options, then wishbone analysis (see Chapter 3) can be used to develop the thinking behind them, from cunning to, hopefully, stunning. Our experience of using the strategic option grid suggests that some options, which do not come out as particularly attractive on first scoring, can turn out to be much more attractive when they are done slightly differently.

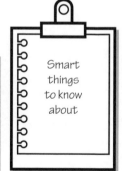

Smart things to know about

THE STRATEGIC OPTION GRID

- It broadens your choices.
- It structures the evaluation.
- It focuses your discussion.
- It is excellent for presentations.
- It can be easily revisited.

## Understanding strategic attractiveness – the GE (General Electric) grid

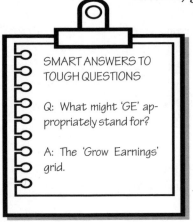
We now need to examine the position of different business units within the growth portfolio. (This can also be done for mini-business units within a larger business). This can be done by using the GE grid, named after General Electric, the successful conglomerate in the US.

The GE grid (see Fig. 4.5) splits positioning into:

• market attractiveness; and

• competitive position.

Market attractiveness combines the main factors:

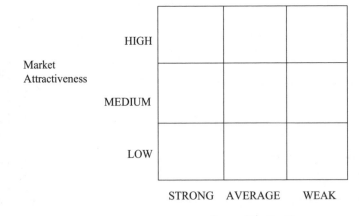

Fig. 4.5   GE grid.

- growth drivers; and

- competitive forces (including the industry mindset).

The GE grid is the primary way of getting behind strategic attractiveness (see our last section), rather than simply short-circuiting and seeing strategic attractions as 'a strategy we focus on doing'. Obviously, you will need to take a view on the relative importance of each of these forces. Here you will need to judge relative importance very much on a case-by-case basis.

Market attractiveness gives an overview of whether a particular market (or segment) offers longer-term financial returns on a par with, greater than, or less than other industries. These 'other industries' are ones which either you are already in or might conceivably enter. Wider still, you can make comparisons with dissimilar industries in which there could be a key factor of production – finance for investment.

Figure 4.5 thus allows the separation of two variables of total market attractiveness from competitive position. The vertical axis depicts 'high', 'medium' or 'low' total market attractiveness. The horizontal axis picks out 'strong', 'average' or 'weak' competitive positions. The GE grid thus enables a multitude of factors to be compared simultaneously.

The GE grid enables you to:

- position an existing growth strategy, having analysed its market attractiveness and competitive position;

- compare it with other growth strategies;

- evaluate new growth opportunities;

- help to reposition an existing business (from right to left on the GE grid, or even diagonally north-west – by shifting the business's market focus) in a turnaround strategy, or by continuous improvement;

- challenge the adequacy of investment to achieve such a repositioning (both long-term investment and revenue costs with longer-term benefits); and

- compare your positioning with other key competitors operating in the same or differing market segments.

To position a business effectively on the GE grid you will also need to take some view of its competitive position. The following ten key criteria will usually suffice (as a checklist).

1 Brand, image and reputation.

2 Simplicity of product/market focus, or alternatively a relevant and broad offering.

3 Relative market (or niche) share.

4 Product and service performance.

5 Distribution channels.

Smart
things
to know
about

---

THE GE GRID

- It is not simplistic – and doesn't just focus on narrow variables like growth rate and market share.
- It is dynamic.
- It prioritizes existing and potential businesses.

---

6   Cost base.

7   Responsiveness (but this doesn't mean reactiveness).

8   Technical and non-technical competencies.

9   Financial strength.

10  Management skills.

Later in this chapter we examine how the customer-facing part of this process can be evaluated, using 'motivator and hygiene factor' analysis.

Besides looking at current competitive advantage, we also need to consider its sustainability. A key task is to protect competitive advantage once this has been gained, as we saw with the Dyson case in Chapter 3. The danger is that competitive advantage is regarded as a 'thing' that you create and then maintain or develop.

## Exercise – the GE grid

Using the above criteria, where would you position one or more of your business areas on the GE grid? What is the 'so what?' from this, especially in terms of potential options for repositioning the business, and its benefits and costs?

To summarize, the key benefits of the GE grid are that it:

* helps to understand present financial performance and to predict future performance;

- scopes the amount of investment to protect and develop the business;

- can help provoke innovative strategies for changing the industry's mind-set;

- helps to prioritize strategic decision making and resource allocation; and

- helps in re-evaluating existing business units.

The GE grid can also be used at a personal level for:

- analysing job attractiveness; and

- analysing your own competitive position (either for getting that next job or for actually doing it after you have got it).

## BMW's strategic options – a short case study

As we saw in the last section, the GE grid is a way of 'helicoptering' over your growth strategies (both present and potential). It also helps us to map these in order to understand their priorities, their upsides and their vulner-abilities.

The GE grid answers the questions:

- 'which businesses are in the most inherently attractive markets?'; and

- 'what businesses have the strongest competitive positions?'

It can be applied to organic growth strategies and to other routes to growth, including acquisitions and alliances.

The GE grid is used for a number of applications relevant to acquisitions, as follows.

- First, to get a better fix on your own strategic position, as a prelude to looking at acquisitions and other options. This is split down by product/ market segment.

- Second, to analyse and evaluate the strategic position of a target acquisition, and especially to:
  - compare and contrast it vis-à-vis your own strategic position – is there overall consistency between both business portfolios?;
  - explore whether acquisition integration can materially reposition any of these businesses, particularly in terms of relative competitive position;
  - understand the basis of economic profit generation in the target's business and to challenge whether this is likely to be sustainable; and
  - understand how much effort in integration and investment may be required to reposition the required business in order to improve its economic profit.

The GE grid is the best way of probing assumed strategic attractiveness in the strategic option grid, which we saw earlier. The significance of the positions on the GE grid (in broad terms) is as follows.

- North-west position – a major generator of economic profit.

- South-west position – a significant generator of economic profit, but with constant struggle.

- North-east position – a marginal generator of economic profit.

- Due-south position – a mixture between just breaking even in economic profit and some dilution of economic profit.

- South-east position – significant, if not major, shareholder value dilution.

A step-by-step worked example for the GE grid is now taken from the acquisition of Rover Group by BMW.

### BMW's strategic position – 1994

BMW was a very successful company that has exploited important niches in the car market with a very strong differentiation strategy. Originally renowned for its quality motorcycles after the Second World War, it then diversified into small cars. Although once regarded as the poor relation to Mercedes, BMW had actually reached a position on a par with (and some could say ahead of) Mercedes. In late 1994 BMW displaced Mercedes as the supplier of engines to the next generation of Rolls-Royce cars.

BMW had built a very impressive brand by 1994. This was established by very clear market positioning, a very high quality product and service from its dealer network to match. The very success of BMW meant, however, that it had become a prime target for competitors to emulate, possibly by moving into direct attack.

BMW's strategic position in 1994 was relatively strong, with its very strong marque, premium prices, dealer network and its relative quality levels. But was BMW (as of the mid-1990s) capable of sustaining its competitive position against competitor attack from both Western and Far-Eastern sources (such as Toyota's Lexus marque)?

There were some symptoms that led to a turning point in BMW's strategic health, around the early 1990s. First, BMW's reputation for quality had not been unblemished. Certain of the early 3-series models in the early 1990s had significant quality problems. But besides the increasing threat of competition, BMW was moving in the direction of medium- and smaller-sized cars. Although BMW sold a lot more of the 3-series than the 5-series, and also a lot more of the 5-series than the 7-series, it was actually the top-of-the-range cars which were rated as outstanding by motoring magazines. So was this a move to downsize a strategic temptation that would ultimately weaken BMW? Also, the competitive forces traditionally tended to be more acutely adverse when one considered the volume end of the car market.

But even before BMW had actively considered buying Rover, it had decided to experiment with the smaller end of medium-sized cars, with its BMW *Compact*, launched in 1994. So BMW *did* have organic options to its acquisitive strategy for Rover Group, at around 1994. Summarizing BMW's strategic position as at 1994, it had:

- been (and still was) a very successful company, which had achieved market leadership in executive, high-performance cars in Europe;

- a worldwide reputation for quality, which is now being imitated by a variety of players; and

- a product line that was beginning to appear out of synchronization with the changing market environment, and that appeared somewhat limited and perhaps over-focused.

It is now worthwhile for you (the reader) to spend some time pondering what other options were available to BMW.

## Exercise – BMW's strategic options

What options were available to BMW (as at 1994) – other than to acquire Rover as a central plank of its strategic development – and how attractive are these? You may wish to explore, for instance:

- strategic alliances;

- organic development (of new products) to broaden its range;

- other acquisition options;

- specific migrating of its competitive strategy to have less emphasis (or even more emphasis) on differentiation;

- maintaining and protecting its current niche position; and

- exploiting new technologies for engine and vehicle design.

Specific options which you might have come up with are: to acquire Porsche, or Volvo, or to merge with VW-Audi (or perhaps a partnership with VW-Audi), or for BMW to set up its own four-wheel-drive business or apply its engine technology in other markets (such as boats, public transport, etc.). How attractive are these options now on the strategic option grid?

Having analysed BMW with considerable depth, we now turn to Rover Group. To understand more about a company's competitive position, we need to establish how much value (perceived and real) it adds to its target

*Smart quotes*

customers – and relative to its key competitors. This leads us on now to a further growth analysis technique – of motivators and hygiene factors.

## Customer value – the motivators and hygiene factors

An important clue in resolving problems of measuring value is the distinction between motivators and hygiene factors. This also enables us to explore the dynamics of value capture. (The idea of motivators and hygiene factors comes from Hertzberg's theory of motivation.)

Hygiene factors are the basic standards of product and service delivery which, unless delivered well, will create value destruction. Where hygiene factors are not met, they detract from value – and from the buying impulse. Equally, some activities may detract from the core delivery of value. Motivator activities excite customers distinctively and are the sources of differentiation. One way of distinguishing motivator activities from hygiene activities is to adapt force-field analysis to the task.

In Fig. 4.6 the conventional 'enabling' forces become the motivators, and the 'constraining' forces become the unmet hygiene factors (and therefore

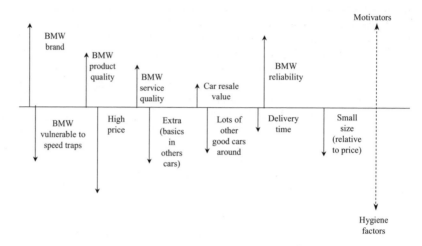

**Fig. 4.6**  Motivator-hygiene factor analysis – businessman contemplating a BMW purchase.

distractors). The relative size of the arrow (or vector) is a visual indication of the actual strength of indicators and hygiene factors (from a customer's perspective). This tool can be used either to help predict customer buying behaviour or to perform customer benchmarking of value added by the firm.

## Not-so-smart approach to hygiene factors

In 2001 I returned my video to an electrical retailer called Asteroid because it: (a) periodically lost all of its TV settings; and (b) lacked a visual display of where it was (in time) on the tape. I was over the 28-days limit for returns imposed by Asteroid. Unimpressed by my protestations, a representative told me: 'Dr Grundy, even if you were a granny who could now not tape her favourite TV programme, the answer would be the same – NO – we cannot replace this with another model. You will have to get it repaired.'

What you will therefore need to think through are the following questions.

1   Is the factor really a motivator or merely a hygiene factor (often managers put into the motivators category things which are simply hygiene factors met to different degrees)?

2   How important is that motivator or hygiene factor?

3   How well is it met (or not met)?

Notice the need to break down points 2 and 3.

Obviously, at some point, motivator-hygiene factor analysis needs to be checked out by some empirical research – with customers. The pattern of motivators and hygiene factors is specific to a customer (in relation to a particular supplier). As this pattern alters considerably, even between individual customers, this explains why, even when a firm offers a very high use-value but at a relatively low price, some customers will still buy from elsewhere. It also underlines the importance of building and reinforcing customer-specific motivator activities – to discourage switching.

Where it is not practicable to collect market data until late on, another technique is to perform 'psychic market research'. This entails asking yourself: 'If we were to ask these questions of this kind of customer – and with my out-of-body experience on full – what can I imagine they would say?' Try this approach sometime – it can prove uncannily accurate, quick and cheap.

Motivator factors are those aspects of customer value which currently:

- are sufficient to cause a customer to switch from an alternative source of supply that is merely average; or

- would make it psychologically difficult or unthinkable to switch to another source of supplier.

Hygiene factors are those aspects of customer value which:

- although insufficient to cause a customer to switch from another source of supply, are quite likely to cause switching behaviour; or

- are frequently the kinds of things which the customer would have potentially paid to avoid them not having been met.

A graphic illustration of unmet hygiene factors is that of the case of the 'Minister for Red Cards'. As a result of very poor customer service in the UK, the author occasionally has cause to issue a Red Card for poor service or products. In this situation he proposes to remedy this in an important new post (N.B. these were actual letters, written in 2001).

*Mr Tony Blair*
*UK Prime Minister*
*10 Downing Street*
*London*
*29 June 2001*

*Dear Tony*

**Minister for Red Cards – a New Cabinet Position**

*I recently came back from an important business trip to Croatia on Tuesday 26th June. Arriving at Heathrow, Terminal 2 at 10 p.m. I was amazed to find passport control heaving with non-UK citizens trying to get into the UK.*

*   UK passport holders were able to easily circumvent the half-hour queues suffered by our visitors, who no doubt had ignored warnings about foot and mouth disease.*

*   I felt impelled to give HM Passport Control a RED CARD, attracting great applause from around 200 tourists. I apologized for this very poor customer*

*service on your personal behalf – and the applause then intensified.*

*As I escaped myself, I realised that the UK needed (and desperately) a new and important catalyst – a Minister for Red Cards. The purpose of this role would be to encourage UK competitiveness in the service economy (both private and public). I am sure that Gordon would approve.*

*If you are interested in making an early appointment I could e-mail you my CV which is very impressive.*

*Yours sincerely*

*Tony Grundy*

*PS. Following recent cabinet salary raises, I am sure I could cope with a slight drop in earnings.*

*PPS. This would make up for my disappointment of not getting the job of coach to the England football team, presumably on account of my being English.*

* * *

*Dr Tony Grundy*
*16 Poets Gate*
*Cheshunt*
*Waltham Cross*
*Herts*
*EN7 6SB*
*6th July 2001*

*Dear Dr Grundy*

*The Prime Minister has asked me to thank you for your recent letter.*

*Mr Blair receives thousands of letters each week and hopes you will understand that, as the matter you raise is the responsibility of the Home Office, he has asked that your letter be forwarded to the Department so that*

*they may reply to you on his behalf.*
*Yours sincerely*

*Mrs T Sampson*

DEALING WITH CALL CENTRES: TURNING TIME-WASTERS TO YOUR OWN ADVANTAGE

After reading that the average consumer spends about 45 hours a year waiting for service from call centres, I decided to teach them a lesson. (At a national cost of £30 an hour, this would represent a time-cost of £1350, and telephone costs of probably £150, totalling £1500.)

So my policy for time-wasters is:

- they are given a YELLOW card after three minutes;
- after six minutes they get a RED card; and
- after nine minutes I then pretend to be my own call centre, keeping them waiting with the following: 'Hello, this is Tony Grundy's call centre. I am sorry that I cannot answer my line currently. But if you would please wait patiently one of my operators will be with you very soon. Naturally, we are unable to say when this will occur, because our main goal is increasing our own operational efficiency, reducing costs and increasing our profits. We apologize for any customer value we have destroyed.'

The author encourages you to try this out. (If this spreads, we could perhaps destroy call centres altogether.)

*Exercise – motivator-hygiene factors*

For one of the above areas of application:

- what are the key motivator and hygiene factors which are unmet (given present delivery competence)?

- how could these factors now be met differently?

The benefits of motivator-hygiene factor analysis are that it:

- gives you an outside-in perspective on your competitive advantage;

- prioritizes customer value, both in terms of importance and the extent to which value is being created (or, indeed, destroyed);

- allows you to think ahead about *future* value creation in the industry, thus pre-empting your competitors; and

- gives some feed-in to your horizontal positioning (i.e. your competitive position) on the GE grid.

Its 'dis-benefits' might include that it can become too subjective unless one is fully capable of having the 'out-of-body experience', and unless some market data is collected.

Having looked at customer value and motivator-hygiene factors in some depth, it is now time to turn to competitor profiling and competitor analysis.

## Competitor profiling and competitor analysis

Competitive profiling and competitor analysis help you to assess how well you are competing vis-à-vis specific competitors. The various aspects of competitive advantage can be scored as 'strong', 'average' or 'weak' or alternatively on a scale of 1–5 points, with 5 being 'very strong' and 1 being 'very weak'. Figure 4.7 contains some generic bases for competing, which have been implemented successfully in over 100 companies. Despite this success, it is important however to tailor these to what is important to your own particular situation. The relative importance of the factors can be assessed by weighting some factors as being more important than others. This analysis needs to be done relative to one or more key competitors, otherwise it is prone to subjectivity.

As an example of more specific competitive strengths, a major international hotel chain identified the following specific dimensions:

|  | Very strong 5 | Strong 4 | Average 3 | Weak 2 | Very weak 1 |
|---|---|---|---|---|---|
| Brand image |  |  |  |  |  |
| Product performance |  |  |  |  |  |
| Service quality |  |  |  |  |  |
| Innovation drive |  |  |  |  |  |
| Cost base |  |  |  |  |  |
| Supporting systems |  |  |  |  |  |
| Support skills |  |  |  |  |  |

Fig. 4.7  Competitor profiling.

- brand name and service reputation;

- locations;

- booking systems and services;

- reception service;

- ancillary facilities;

- room quality;

- food (and beverages) quality;

- cost base; and

- personalized customer service.

Specific criteria can be derived (indirectly) from environmental analysis (especially the external growth drivers and the five competitive forces) and also from customer value (or motivator-hygiene factor) analysis. The other major thing to consider is the analysis of factors impacting on costs.

Below are some useful pointers to adding a more objective bite to the analysis.

- For aspects of *perceived* superior value – test out whether particular customers or market segments *do* actually perceive you as superior to a particular competitor.

- For *actual* value (of product or service) – analyse the dimensions of this value and compare on a line-for-line basis with a key competitor.

When doing this it is vital (once you have listed out your factors) to ask the question: 'What is the one BIG THING that we have forgotten?' Usually there is one Big Thing – and sometimes this is where you are weak and competitors are strong. In interpreting the criteria in Fig. 4.7, the following points are worth reflecting on.

- Brand strength – this is not just about brand awareness, but whether this is perceived as an attractive brand halo by customers.

- Product performance and value – this focuses on the perceived value for money of the core product.

- Innovation effectiveness – this is not just about being innovative, but actually delivering real results from it, either through adding more value to customers or reducing costs, or being able to develop strategically more rapidly.

- Systems – these are the IT and non-IT routine processes for delivering value through the organization.

- Skills base – this comprises general management, commercial, financial, marketing and sales, operations, IT and HR skills.

Competitor profiling can be used for:

- identifying specific growth breakthroughs (to attack competitors);

- acquisitions;

- alliances (to help assess complementary and relative strength); and

- market entry strategies.

And, more specifically, to:

- help position your business portfolio on the GE grid (making it less subjective); and

- challenge internal patterns of resource allocation (you may be competitively weak in an underfunded area).

## Exercise – competitor profiling

For one key competitor of interest, consider the following.

- Where are they positioned on the competitor profile?

- Where are you positioned?

- What is the 'so what?' from this; for example, in terms of:
  - overall positioning and relative vulnerability; and/or
  - possible strategic breakthroughs for your company?

The choice of which competitor(s) to analyse is an interesting issue in itself. This choice is very far from being self-evident. You can choose the competitors to examine based on:

- likely threat;

- ease of attack; or

- potential to learn from them.

It may be useful to target a competitor (or new entrant) on the basis of these criteria *and* the degree of your ignorance – although it may seem to be a bad idea to analyse a competitor who you know relatively little about, this can be highly illuminating. It is also especially interesting to draw up the profile of a new entrant.

When displaying the positions of competitors, do please avoid putting more than two competitors on the grid at once. Even three competitors can become visually difficult and confusing. A practical tip here is to use a blank acetate with the competitor profile format on. You then create (using a blank acetate and a felt pen) zigzag pictures for each competitor, in different colours. By overlaying any two competitors on the standard acetate you can mix and match the positionings. It is crucial to do your competitors first, because otherwise you may be biased by perceptions about your own positioning.

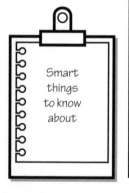

Smart
things
to know
about

OPTIONS FOR GROWTH

1 You should concentrate on a relatively small number of growth break-throughs.
2 To be creative you need to create lines of enquiry; for example, by changing the rules of the industry, by having out-of-body experiences (of being a customer) or through the 'alien' approach.
3 The octopus grid helps to structure and broaden your choice of options.
4 The strategic option grid helps broaden your options, and to appraise systematically their attractiveness.
5 It also helps you to focus on critical uncertainties and to prioritize any data collection.
6 The GE grid helps to perform a more objective appraisal of strategic attractiveness.
7 Motivators and hygiene factors and competitor profiling help give a more accurate GE grid positioning – in terms of competitive positioning.

# 5

# Managing Organic Growth – With Success

## Introduction

We have already given you a number of aspects of the growth process. In particular, we looked at the strategy mix, as a way of understanding the particular phase that a growth strategy is at. Next, we examined the growth

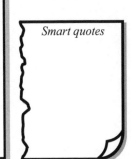

Growth – the importance of process

'What is interesting here is that because people do seem to target the value of what is coming out of a strategic thought, they probably don't have them in the first place or, when they do have them, they are intoxicated by the ideas stream and do not get into the almost carnivorous role of thinking what value can you get out of them. Maybe one should cut down the number of strategic thoughts so that we can get more focus.'

Tony Grundy, Cranfield School of Management

cycle, which helped us to understand the cyclical and evolutionary characteristics of growth. We also looked (in Chapter 1) at the following phases of managing growth, on which we now expand a little to cover:

- growth diagnosis;

- growth options;

- growth strategy and plans;

- implementation; and

- review and control.

The growth diagnosis phase involves:

- diagnosing the external and internal growth drivers of the business;

- assessing the quality of growth, given the five competitive forces;

- understanding current and prospective strategic positioning with the GE grid; and

- diagnosing internal and external problems or constraints using fishbone analysis.

The growth options phase entails:

- using the octopus grid and the creative lines of enquiry in Chapter 4 to generate new options for growth; and

- applying the strategic option grid (and supporting techniques, as necessary) to evaluate options.

The growth strategy and plans phase involves:

- using wishbone analysis and the uncertainty grids to flesh out the strategy; and

- applying 'from-to' ('FT') analysis, how-how analysis, AID analysis and value and cost driver analysis, in order to create business plans.

The implementation phase entails:

- understanding difficulty using force-field analysis (perhaps with the difficulty-over-time curve); and

- exploring stakeholder influences using stakeholder analysis (and stakeholder agenda analysis).

The review and control phase invites:

- diagnosis of failures and disappointments with fishbone analysis; and

- analysis of successes and near-successes with wishbone analysis.

The various phases of the growth process can be actively facilitated, which brings us to the role of the growth facilitator and of growth workshops.

> *Smart quotes*
>
> 'It is very difficult to allocate the success of an organization to a particular type of thing, to a particular strategy. Success comes from a whole host of reasons. In my view, planning per se does not necessarily help. I think insights are very much more important than any planning process.'
>
> Cliff Bowman, Cranfield School of Management

## Growth facilitators and growth workshops

In this chapter we examine:

- the role of the growth facilitator;

- running effective growth workshops;

- the importance of organizational capability; and

- organic growth in the football industry.

The key ways in which the growth facilitator can add to the strategy value include the following 13 activities.

1 Acting as an independent sounding board.

2 Helping to set the strategic agenda.

3 Asking the right questions.

4 Asking the questions that others dare not ask.

5 Providing a process for thinking.

6 Collecting and interpreting data.

7 Facilitating the thinking process.

8 Generating or providing the teams with 'out-of-the-box' ideas.

9 Acting as a catalyst for decision making and for action.

10  Constructively critiquing the output.

11  Helping identify blind spots.

12  Providing energy and enthusiasm.

13  Being a symbolic presence – to help people think and
behave differently.

Some of the above activities may seem relatively self-
evident – like 'Providing a process for thinking' or
'Collecting and interpreting data'. Others might be less
obvious, such as the latter two points of providing energy
and enthusiasm, and being a symbolic presence. Being a
symbolic presence involves value being added simply by
being there. This presence sends signals that something different can happen and that it can happen during the session.

Also, note that some facilitators (often external consultants) will focus on a
relatively small number of the above activities – for example, on collecting
and interpreting data. But sometimes consultants work principally as process consultants. This means that they primarily add value by facilitating

'There is the style of the facilitator and the process – do these actually
fit? Do they want to listen? And the process also includes how people
have been asked to come to the event, how has permission been reflected
in how people have been asked to come to the event. And it depends on
whether he (the leader) stops and says, "I trust you" and goes away, or
whether he stays and is empowering.'

Phil Davies, Cranfield School of Management

the strategic thinking process. This is in contrast to the *expert* consultant, who is hired primarily because of their content expertise.

All of the 13 roles of the growth facilitator can be exercised by an internal manager, albeit sometimes with greater difficulty. The activities which might be harder to fulfil for an internal manager are:

- asking the questions that others dare not to ask;

- critiquing the output – and constructively; and

- being a symbolic presence.

Whilst not impossible, the challenge is perhaps greater for the internal facilitator in the above. This challenge puts more stress on the internal facilitator's self-confidence, and indeed on their courage. Depending upon the sensitivity of the situation, this may mean that the internal growth facilitator may need to put the process first and thoughts about their longer-term career in the organization second. Success in this role can be the ideal preparation for becoming a top manager. Also, if a manager succeeds in this difficult role, then there should be no shortage of job offers elsewhere!

Besides playing an official (internal) facilitator role, every manager can also adopt this role by stealth or informally. Consultancy facilitation ought to be an integral part of a senior manager's skill-set.

To check out whether you have the natural capability to become an internal growth consultant (whether formally or informally), now answer the brief (twelve-question) questionnaire in Table 5.1.

**Table 5.1** Internal growth consultant questionnaire.

|  | Very strong (5) | Strong (4) | Average (3) | Weak (2) | Very weak (1) |
|---|---|---|---|---|---|
| What is my natural ability to see the very big picture? |  |  |  |  |  |
| What is my ability to think outside the box? |  |  |  |  |  |
| What is my ability in devising management processes? |  |  |  |  |  |
| What is my level of political skills? |  |  |  |  |  |
| What is my level of interpersonal skills – at senior levels? |  |  |  |  |  |
| What is my ability at asking the right questions – and at the right time? |  |  |  |  |  |
| What is my listening skills ability – and my powers of observation? |  |  |  |  |  |
| What is my ability to cope with the ambiguous and uncertain? |  |  |  |  |  |
| What is my ability to handle personal stress under a difficult challenge? |  |  |  |  |  |
| What is the level of my all-round analytical ability? |  |  |  |  |  |
| What is the level of my communication ability? |  |  |  |  |  |
| What is the level of my own persistence and drive? |  |  |  |  |  |
| **Total score** |  |  |  |  |  |

Now calculate your overall score out of 60.

- Score 55–60: You might consider setting up your own consultancy (after some internal experience or with another firm).

- Score 45–54: This may be a full-time internal role for you.

- Score 35–44: You can add a lot of value merely through internal consulting by stealth.

- Score 25–34: Don't give up! Work out a number of developmental activities to move this forward (especially pinpointing key projects or meetings as the vehicle for consultancy-by-stealth).

We now give you some very practical advice on designing, running and getting maximum value out of growth workshops.

Although workshops can generate disproportionate value (and vision), this can be diluted considerably where:

- there is inadequate pre-planning (of issues, process and outputs);

*Smart quotes*

Running Effective Growth Workshops

'You need to have all the right people there, so they will become brought into the thinking actually at the time that it happens. And they tend to share the enthusiasm more than if it is an idea that happens at a meeting where only one or two people are present, and then you have to go through the experience of selling it and repeating the thought processes. Often that makes it die a bit; it loses spontaneity.'

Jo Ranger, ZIFA Life

- there is no facilitation, or where it is ineffective;

- there are no plans in place to deal with the output and to move it on into the next phase; or

- there are no tools to help managers make progress (use the tools contained in this book).

## Twelve questions on how to run a growth workshop

Twelve key questions on how to run a growth workshop are as follows.

1  What is the objective of the growth workshop?

2  How does it relate to other initiatives?

3  What are seen as the key outputs (learning, problem definition, action plans, behavioural shift, etc.), and how will these be documented and communicated, and to whom?

4  Who needs to be involved?

5  How will it be positioned in the organization and by whom?

6  Who will facilitate, and are they seen as competent and impartial?

7  Where should it be held and what facilities are required?

8  What are the next steps following the workshop likely to be?

9 What key barriers and blockages may arise, and how will these be dealt with, and by whom?

10 What specific activities will be undertaken and what will this input require?

11 How will these be broken down into discussion groups and who will be in each one?

12 How long is required to make substantial progress on each issue and what happens if tasks are incomplete?

Experience shows that it is essential to consider all these questions at length, rather than rushing into a workshop on a particular issue with merely a broad agenda. The questions emphasize both content and process, and involve thinking through how these interrelate. They also involve analysing both current and future context – this provides high quality feed-in of data, and also helps to think through feedback into the management process in detail and in advance.

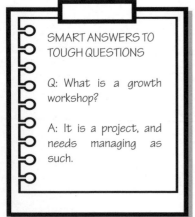

It is vital to structure the content of each workshop to contain some key questions, which will structure the session. An example of questions to choose from is given below.

*Growth questions for a workshop – example*

For one area of your growth strategy, consider the following questions.

1 Where this is a problem, what are its root causes (fishbone analysis)?

'One of the things that could be done to improve the quality of strategic thinking is to improve the physiological and physical aspects of it. It sounds a really obvious point. People ought to be rested, they should not bring their mobile phones with them, they should feel that they are ready to focus. I take them for a walk outdoors [elaborates].'

Phil Davies, Cranfield School of Management

2   Where this is an opportunity, what is its vision and also what factors (both within and outside your control or influence) would need to line up to deliver this vision?

3   For this breakthrough, what is its targeted, economic value? (Think about its likely net cashflows into the future.)

4   Where the breakthrough comprises a number of discretionary actions or activities, where are these positioned on the attractiveness/ implementation-difficulty (AID) grid? (See Chapter 7.)

5   What is your cunning plan now for implementing it?

6   How difficult will it be to implement (force-field analysis)? (See Chapter 7.)

7   Who are the key stakeholders involved during the lifetime of this breakthrough?

8   Where are these stakeholders likely to be positioned, given your cunning plan, in terms of attitude (for, neutral or against) and influence (high, medium or low)? (See Chapter 7.)

9 How do these patterns of attitude and influence shift for different areas of implementation? (Here you might need to do separate stakeholder agenda analyses for each action or sub-project.)

10 Given the agendas of key stakeholders (use stakeholder agenda analysis), how might you influence them either to be more favourable or to reduce the influence of those who are against?

11 Given all of this thinking, what scenario stories can you tell about the implementation:
   • going very smoothly;
   • being somewhat turbulent; or
   • going completely wrong?

N.B. You will need to tailor these questions to your own situation.

Finally, to help head off internal barriers to the workshop, and to avoid undue contention and disruption, it is suggested that you use the 'P' behaviours (see Growth Workshops box).

In the remainder of this chapter we cover the importance of organic capability. We then turn to an example of outstandingly successful organic growth: Manchester United and the football industry.

## The importance of organizational capability

Any organization's existing capability and constraints in this capacity can act as a major brake on growth. Even if the company *actually does* grow, it can overstretch itself and begin to suffer organizational burn-out. This may

GROWTH WORKSHOPS – THE 'P' BEHAVIOURS

When beginning a growth workshop, one should ask all participants to brain-storm the 'P' behaviours that we want to avoid. To add some humour and reality, anyone caught behaving in a 'P'-type fashion is asked to contribute £1 to the facilitator's or chairman's favourite charity. A list of possible 'P'-behaviours is:

- political;
- parochial;
- procrastinating;
- posturing;
- protectionist;
- pretending;
- pessimistic;
- petty;
- preservation.

The real value of the 'P' process tool is that you rarely have to use it during a workshop if you have got people to buy into it up-front.

manifest quite rapidly through losing customers or through disenchanted managers leaving.

At Manchester United, for example, a major issue (as of 2001) was who would succeed its manager, Sir Alex Ferguson, who was due to retire at the end of the 2001–2 season. Clearly the choice of a replacement manager will be a decisive factor in determining whether or not United continue to domi-nate UK football and to compete for winning the Champions League.

Indeed, succession issues are often crucial in growth – and are often ducked because of their difficulty and inevitable sensitivity. Techniques for thinking about succession include the following.

- Wishbone analysis – what is your vision of the capabilities of a new leader, and what would have to line up to: (a) find them; (b) acquire them; and (c) keep them?

- The strategic option grid – for appraising different succession options.

- Force-field analysis – for thinking through how easy or difficult it would be to integrate a successor.

- Scenario storytelling and the uncertainty grids – to consider the potential vulnerability of the handover (and its aftermath).

In addition to succession issues, a number of other organizational issues with an impact on growth can be addressed using the growth techniques. These include:

- organizational weaknesses (internal growth brakes) – these can be diagnosed using fishbone analysis and prioritized through AID analysis, prior to being project managed through implementation difficulties (force-field analysis and stakeholder analysis); and

- organizational breakthroughs (for example, management development initiatives, business process re-engineering, or restructuring) – these can be addressed through wishbone analysis and the uncertainty grids.

## Organic growth in the football industry

The football industry is one which has traditionally added value in simple ways. It has now changed into one that is complex, changing the basis of competing and of shareholder value creation, and that has offered unparalleled opportunities for growth. This case study in illustration is set out as follows:

- the industry context; and

- Manchester United – the case.

The industry context also offers the opportunity to review and reinforce the learning from Porter's five competitive forces.

## The industry context

Association football ('soccer') is the most popular spectator sport in Britain, with six times more attendance than the next most popular sports – greyhound racing and horseracing. Football is also received with similar enthusiasm in many European countries – and indeed worldwide – where frequently the level of excitement generated exceeds even that in the UK.

Summarizing Porter's five forces analysis for the football industry, we see the following.

- Buyers have relatively low bargaining power (as their loyalty to clubs in traditional customer segments is usually very high). This loyalty is now breaking down as an increasing proportion of followers watch different teams. This force historically supports above-normal value creation in the industry, but this effect may disappear.

- Suppliers do have considerable (high) bargaining power – these suppliers being particularly the players. Players' salaries absorb typically over half of gate-takings, and high-performing players command considerable transfer fees. This force may thus undermine value creation in the industry.

- Substitutes are an important threat. We include here direct substitutes, such as other leisure activities, besides indirect substitutes, such as watching games on satellite television. This force thus poses a growing threat to value creation.

- Competitive rivalry – oddly there is not typically an intense rivalry for fans on a local basis, although rivalry on the pitch is high. The 'rivalry' force does not act to depress industry profits in a serious way. This force thus plays a neutral, or even positive, role in supporting value creation.

This competitive forces analysis suggests that, although the competitive environment generally supports a super-normal value creation in the industry, there are significant longer-term threats to this. Football has therefore now developed from its traditional base of taking receipts for the game to become a much more complex set of business activities – for example, sponsorship, advertising, television, merchandising, conferences and catering – thereby extending its value domain.

Football has thus been transformed from an industry with relatively low value creation (in the early 1990s) to one with high value creation to this present time – for Premier League clubs. By migrating the way in which value has been created in the industry, Manchester United has achieved extraordinary returns for its shareholders.

So let us now turn to the specific case of Manchester United.

## Manchester United

Manchester United has been a very successful football club for several decades. It has thrived despite setbacks – for example, the Munich air-crash

around 30 years ago, which effectively wiped out the team. In the 1960s it spawned players like Bobby Charlton and George Best, and under Alex Ferguson, its manager, it has rekindled this success in the 1990s. Manchester United has been instrumental in changing the game from being primarily a spectator activity to a mass, market-based product. This has transformed its financial results.

Financial analysis of the breakdown of the club's turnover during the early 1990s highlights how the industry – and in particular Manchester United – dramatically changed its ability to generate value. Table 5.2 shows how the revenue of Manchester United grew since 1989 – all categories of rev-

**Table 5.2**  Manchester United revenues 1989–1995.

|                     | 1989 £m 9 | 1990 £m 12 | 1993 £m 23 | 1994 £m 42 | 1995 £m 61 |
|---------------------|-----------|------------|------------|------------|------------|
| **Made up of (%):** |           |            |            |            |            |
| Television          | 8         | 6          | 15         | 10         | 11         |
| Sponsorship         | 19        | 16         | 15         | 11         | 12         |
| Conference/catering | 8         | 7          | 8          | 16         | 18         |
| Merchandising       | 7         | 20         | 21         | 23         | 27         |
| Gate receipts       | 58        | 51         | 49         | 40         | 32         |

enue have grown but that from merchandising has increased the greatest. By 1999, profits stood at £20mn.

Recent statistics for Manchester United are shown in Table 5.3 below.

**Table 5.3**   Manchester United 1996–2000 (for years ended 31 July; figures in £000).

|  | 2000 | 1999 | 1998 | 1997 | 1996 |
|---|---|---|---|---|---|
| Turnover | 116,005 | 110,674 | 87,875 | 87,939 | 53,316 |
| Operating profit before amortization of players and exceptional item | 30,073 | 32,310 | 26,996 | 26,201 | 14,167 |
| Amortization of players | (13,092) | (10,192) | (4,723) | — | — |
| Exceptional item | (1,300) | (1,807) | — | — | 2,173 |
| Operating profit | 15,681 | 20,311 | 22,273 | 26,201 | 16,340 |
| Share of other items | — | — | — | (982) | (1,777) |
| Total operating profit (Group and share of joint venture and associate) | 14,699 | 18,534 | 22,273 | 26,201 | 16,340 |
| Profit on disposal of players | 1,633 | 2,193 | 2,947 | — | — |
| Net transfer fees | — | — | — | 293 | (1,300) |
| Net interest receivable | 456 | 1,684 | 2,619 | 1,083 | 359 |
| Profit on ordinary activities before taxation | 16,788 | 22,411 | 27,839 | 27,577 | 15,399 |
| Taxation | (4,838) | (7,023) | (8,211) | (8,549) | (4,126) |
| Profit for the year | 11,950 | 15,388 | 19,628 | 19,028 | 11,273 |
| Dividends | (4,936) | (4,676) | (4,416) | (4,026) | (3,221) |
| Retained profit for the year | 7,014 | 10,712 | 15,212 | 15,002 | 8,052 |
| Shareholders' funds | 114,950 | 107,936 | 97,132 | 72,148 | 40,762 |

## Value-creating activities

First of all, we look at:

- value creation in the football industry – and at Manchester United;

- industry change and value-creating activities;

- cost drivers and competitiveness; and

- alternatives for future industry change and for Manchester United.

Value is created in any business through the interaction of a number of external and internal factors, which we call the 'business value system' (Grundy 1998). Besides the traditional value-creating activities of fans paying to see their team in action, the years 1994–97 saw a huge growth in football merchandising. This merchandising includes, for instance, Manchester United replica strips, which cost anything from between £30 and £45 for children, up to £60-plus for adult strips. These strips appear to command a considerable premium relative to other fashion items.

We now show how growth can be generated by looking for further, inter-related value-creating activities. This can be done by mapping the system of value-creating criteria called the business value system. A business value system for the successful football clubs is shown in Fig. 5.1. This high-lights the need to maintain match performance as a means of providing the platform for value-creating activities elsewhere. It is precisely because of the interdependencies within this business value system that you cannot naively answer the question of creating activities elsewhere. It is precisely because of the interdependencies within this business value system that you cannot naively answer the question of: 'Exactly where do we make (or lose) money in our [football] business?' (Football, of course, is not unique in this

– most business interdependencies make value measurement very difficult to achieve.)

This question is also linked to the adjacent one of: 'Where (and how) will we make money in the future?' Although this is a question implicit in most treatments of strategy formulation, in practice this question is very much at the forefront of managers' minds.

For example, if we focus once again on the situation of Manchester United, some major pressures on its drive towards game commercialization have emerged. This has provoked a backlash from sections of the traditional fan-base, who have actually demanded seats on the Manchester United board of directors.

Media coverage is likely to prove an increasingly important source of revenue. Manchester United has already set up its own Sky satellite channel.

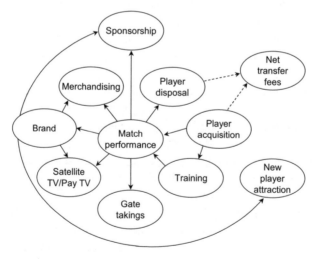

**Fig. 5.1**   Business value system – football clubs.

Also, revenues from European matches increased considerably. This was a major factor that increased the club's market capitalization to a healthy half-a-billion pounds by late 1996.

## Industry change

In the 1990s there has been an undeniably increasing pressure on clubs' costs. The transfer market, for example, is growing fast. By 2001, players were regularly changing hands for over £10mn – Veron costing United over £26mn and Figo costing Real Madrid £41mn.

This trend is continuing, as top clubs compete more for 'big signings', and a higher premium must be paid for star quality. The growing transfer market has also, more importantly, sparked wage rises, and the recent transfer ruling allowing greater freedom of movement for players will accelerate this trend as clubs compete for players with wage levels. Players' earnings rose by around 20% in the mid-1990s, accelerating to 30% per annum more recently.

In parallel with these changes, major investments have been made on grounds, and these have consumed capital. Continued investments will need to be made but there is a danger that certain clubs will 'feel richer' and fuel the transfer market further. Perhaps, at some stage, the 'bubble' will burst, even with revenues fuelled by pay-per-view TV.

We now briefly describe a scenario where pressure mounts on football clubs to revise or moderate their 'commercialization' strategy and they are left with falling revenues and margins at a time of unduly high costs. The likely result: fall-out of weaker clubs (and maybe even financial failure of one or more of the larger clubs is a scenario with at least some plausibility. The 'end-game' here would be – literally – restructuring the game). With its rivals hot on its heels, Manchester United might feel under pressure to sustain the success of recent years.

*Exercise – growth options for Manchester United*

Using the octopus grid, generate a number of strategic options for Manchester United, as of 2001. How attractive are these options on the strategic option grid? For each option, do these scores improve or could you then uplift your option to a cunning, if not a stunning, plan?

Also, think about geographic scope, other media opportunities, football's potential interdependencies with the mobile telecommunications market, etc.

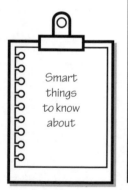

Smart
things
to know
about

---

MANAGING FOR VALUE

- It is impossible to fully appreciate the factors driving an industry – both now and in the future – without an appreciation of both the strategic drivers and how economic value is being created in the business value system.
- In order to identify the possibilities for value migration, work backwards from current and latent customer value. What are the distinctive areas of customer value which might cause a customer to re-evaluate perceived value? And how can a reasonable element of this extra perceived value be captured by the company (for example, through a higher price)?
- Besides asking the question 'How should we grow strategically?' you have to ask – simultaneously – 'Where and how will we be making money?' The notion that economic value analysis 'brings up the rear' – and only follows on from strategic analysis – is a most dangerous and misleading one.
- Effective co-ordination of performance requires a balanced growth strategy, rather than a pursuit of particular financial goals to the exclusion of more indirect impact.
- Truly profitable growth is very much contingent upon creating and preserving an external competitive environment that is conducive to making good returns. This profit/earning potential is then amplified by competitive dominance (as at Manchester United) and is then underpinned by layer upon layer of reinforcing competitive advantage.

---

SUCCESSFUL MANAGEMENT OF ORGANIC GROWTH

1  The growth process is often just as important as dealing with the content of growth issues.
2  This process needs skilful facilitation and 'helicopter' events like awaydays and workshops.
3  These events (and the process) need to be project managed.
4  A series of specific questions needs to be formulated for the process (in advance) to focus discussion.
5  Each workshop needs to be appropriately positioned in the organization.
6  Above almost everything else, inadequate organizational capability is a major cause of growth factors.
7  The Manchester United case gives us a model of how effective organic growth can be pursued in a cunning way – leading to dominance.

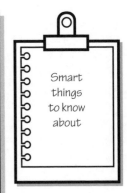

Smart
things
to know
about

# 6
# Managing Acquisitive Growth – With Success

## Introduction

Acquisition is often seen as an accelerated path to growth. But frequently this path ends in tears as the acquisition strategy may not be well thought through, the deal not well managed and the integration process may go badly.

This chapter gives you a process for managing acquisitive growth more effectively. We take you through:

- how acquisitions might add value;

- the acquisition process; and

- Granada versus Forte – a case study.

'Pooh was so busy not looking where he was going that he stepped on a piece of the Forest which had been left out by mistake; and he only just had time to think to himself: "I'm flying. What Owl does. I wonder how you stop ..." when he stopped.

Bump!

"Ow!" squeaked something.

"Help!" said a small, high voice.

"That's me again," thought Pooh. "I've had an Accident, and fallen down a well, and my voice has gone all squeaky and works before I'm ready for it, because I've done something to myself inside ..."

"Help-help!"

"So it must be a very bad Accident.'"

A.A. Milne, *Winnie the Pooh*

## How acquisitions might add value

In this section we look at how the value of acquisitions can be segmented and at the impact of uncertainty.

We have already seen one crude approach to understanding the value of an acquisition using the V1/V2/V3 typology, where:

- V1 is the value inherent in the business strategy itself;

- V2 is the value added through the particular deal; and

Segmenting value

'This tendency toward quantification occurs for several reasons …
Although [analytical] techniques are used in good faith, the assessments
they develop are only estimates. Too often these estimates become precise expectations because they are quantified and they reflect the stated
purpose of the acquisition.'

Haspeslagh & Jemison

- V3 is the value created or destroyed through post-acquisition management.

V1 can be understood more deeply through the GE grid (see Chapter 4). A
number of techniques from that chapter help to provide better support for
understanding current and future value generation, especially the following.

- The growth drivers – for understanding the sustainability of expansion
  in the market or in the company's turnover.

- The five competitive forces – these help in understanding the robustness
  of margins and also to identify shifts in the industry structure, for example through new competitors entering the market or through changes in
  distribution channel strategy.

- The target's competitive position – a weak position might entail considerable future investment.

But there are very many ways of understanding value, which can be ob-
tained by segmenting it in new ways. For example, consider the following
segmentation of value into: future enhancing and protective value; future
opportunity value; synergistic value; and 'sweat value'.

- Enhancing and protective value – the value which can be added either by strengthening the acquired business's current competitive position and scope, or the value to the acquirer of a defensive nature (for instance, in avoiding loss of economies of scale).

- Future opportunity value – the value of the opportunity stream inherent in both the acquired company's markets and its existing platform. This value can come from possible new products, services, network channels or technologies, or simply through fast market growth generally.

- Synergistic value – the value of bringing together particular activities within the business value systems.

- 'Sweat value' – the value released by pure reduction of costs or assets in the acquired company, or the potential disposal of whole businesses.

Here we draw up separate pictures for the major high-level value drivers and also the high-level cost drivers. Figures 6.1 and 6.2 show how this technique was used to understand BMW's acquisition of Rover.

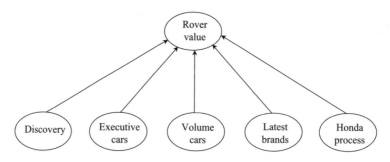

**Fig. 6.1**  Rover's value drivers.

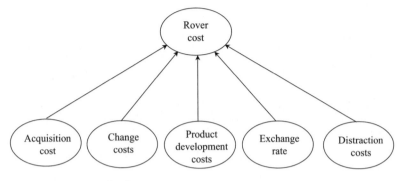

**Fig. 6.2** Rover's cost drivers.

Notice in these figures the dependence of Rover Group on the value generation from the four-wheel-drive *Discovery* model. Also notice the number of
major cost drivers reducing the value generation of Rover (Fig. 6.2). (For
more on value and cost drivers, see Chapter 8.)

### Value, uncertainty and scenarios

Risk and uncertainty analysis for acquisitions should be conducted not by
standard, pre-set sensitivity percentages, but by a deeper appreciation of the
robustness of key variables – the value and cost drivers. To facilitate this,
it is useful to draw upon scenario storytelling (about the future), using the
importance–uncertainty grid (from Chapter 2).

Figure 6.3 uses the methodology for BMW's acquisition of Rover Group.
This shows BMW's assumptions (below) as becoming *both* more important
*and* more uncertain, shifting both south and east.

- Rover's existing product range (volume cars) was reasonably strong.

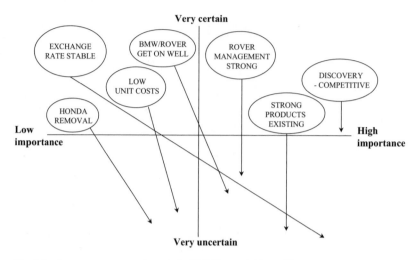

**Fig. 6.3**  Importance–uncertainty grid – BMW's acquisition of Rover.

- The four-wheel-drive *Discovery* model would remain highly competitive.

- Rover's unit costs were reasonably low.

- Rover's dependence on Honda could be removed without doubling or trebling existing investment levels.

- Rover's existing management resources were 'strong'.

- BMW would be able to get on well with Rover's management team.

- The UK exchange rate would not strengthen them by over 20%.

These shifts might have been anticipated before the event (see Grundy, 1995). The effect of these adverse shifts meant that BMW destroyed shareholder value of (according to some sources – see, for example, *The Independent*, 28 March 2001) between £2.5bn and £3bn. Yet at the time, the acquisition of Rover (at around £800mn) was felt to be 'cheap'.

## The value of divestment

Divestment may be relevant from the following two perspectives.

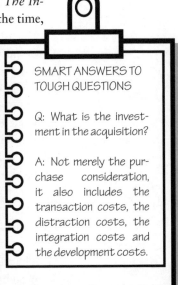

SMART ANSWERS TO TOUGH QUESTIONS

Q: What is the investment in the acquisition?

A: Not merely the purchase consideration, it also includes the transaction costs, the distraction costs, the integration costs and the development costs.

- You may not necessarily wish to retain all the businesses' operations following an acquisition. For example, arguably, BMW should have divested itself of all or part of Rover's volume-car business to concentrate on the four-wheel-drive business and niche cars like the MG. In that event, divestment valuation issues are of parallel interest to acquisition valuation.

- You will not always be the acquirer. Indeed, as we saw earlier, it is usually the vendor who adds value during the acquisition process, not the acquirer.

Even where a business area is profitable and has longer-term potential, the following four questions still need to be asked in the context of corporate development.

1  How much shareholder value can be added by the group parent to this business unit in future?

2  How does this compare with what other corporate parents could add to the business?

3    Could we sell the business to another corporate group for more than what it is worth to us (based on real or perceived market value)?

4    Could we generate incremental shareholder value by reinvesting the proceeds in more exciting opportunities ourselves (and ones which we would be unlikely to be able to fund otherwise)?

Sadly, there is still limited evidence that many managers take fundamental questions like this seriously – until they themselves are subject to a break-up bid. The following checklist should now help you to think through how to get the best value out of divestment.

## Ten lessons for the divesting owners/management

1  What features of the market environment can you emphasize as being attractive (especially the growth drivers)? (V1)

2  What past competitive strengths can you identify and extrapolate out into the future, emphasizing dominance or near-dominance in key segments? (V1)

3  What is your future opportunity stream and what would it be worth as an upside if you had more funds to invest (i.e. from the acquirer)? (V1)

4  How can you create real or imagined rivalry for a deal and which new parent would it be worth most to? (V2)

5  What is the lowest cost of capital that could be used to discount our cashflows (and how could we justify this)? (V2)

6 What is the highest realistic terminal value – at the end of the forecast time horizons – and how can we justify this? (V2)

7 How can we best convey the impression that we are not in a hurry to do a deal (and we might not need to do one anyway)? (V2)

8 What are the particular agendas on the acquisition team's minds (especially personal and political) and how can we exploit 'loose bricks' in the acquisition team's bid strategy? (V2)

9 What synergies with the acquirer's business value system (real or imagined) can you envisage and what 'best value' can be put on these? (V3)

10 What is the best case for achieving 'sweat value' for integration and how can this be built into our plans and forecasts ('we will do it anyway')? (V3)

## The acquisition process

'The acquisition process is frequently described as having a "life of its own" characterized by alternating periods of waiting and frenetic activity. As the tension, pace, and involvement rise relentlessly, participants tend to feel unable to stop the acquisition process or even to slow its tempo. This sense of inexorable momentum contrasts sharply with the traditional portrayal of acquisitions as carefully calculated strategic acts.'

Haspeslagh & Jemison, *Managing Acquisitions*

*Smart quotes*

Figure 6.4 outlines the acquisition process in five key stages, as follows.

**Fig. 6.4** The acquisition process.

1 Strategy and objectives – unless an acquirer is very clear about its current strategic position and intent, the acquisition may have a spurious fit to the acquirer's goals.

2 Search – unless very clear criteria are set for screening acquisition targets (strategic 'dos' and 'don'ts'), the search process will be unfocused and misdirected.

3 Evaluation – this demands both qualitative and quantitative analysis to link the perspectives of strategy, marketing operations, organization and finance.

4 Deal-making – although this is a crucial part of the process, it is only one of the stages when things can go right or wrong. Also, during the deal-making process the strategic assumptions coming out of the first two stages will need extensive checking-out.

5 Integration (or post-acquisition management) and learning – during this phase any changes to management, operations or strategy are implemented and there is further development via new opportunities or harvesting synergies.

Ten critical success factors for the acquisition process (with which you should now match up your current situation) are likely to be as follows.

1 You are very clear as a management team what your strategic goals are – and what your own current strategic position is.

2 You are not doing it for the wrong reasons (for example, the pure pursuit of growth, sheer ambition, excitement, prestige, etc.).

3 The acquisition team project manager shows strong, clear leadership throughout the process.

4 Other options are not closed down prematurely (for example, organic development, alliances or other acquisitions).

5 The team has a balanced mix of skills and can (as a whole) manage all the perspectives of strategic, financial, organizational, tax and legal.

6 The team is sufficiently experienced (in managing acquisitions) and is not learning 'on the job'.

7 The team has enough spare time and capacity to devote to the process – without undermining their present jobs.

8 The team does not succumb to the thrill or the pressure of the acquisition chase.

9 Rivalry for the target (from other buyers) is not so high that V2 (the value generated, diluted or destroyed by the deal) becomes negative.

10 In the urge to accomplish a deal you do not miss the 'One Big Thing', which is not so obvious and which could materially hamper the success of the acquisition.

## The acquisition strategy

KILLER QUESTIONS

How well has your organization managed the ten critical success factors of the acquisition process in the past?

Where acquisitions are concerned, it is extremely dangerous to have an open, or 'emergent', strategy. In order to capture shareholder value from an acquisition it is imperative to have a strategy which is primarily 'deliberate'. A deliberate strategy is one where 'there is a clear, deliberate and detailed plan of achieving our goals – and with competitive advantage'. For acquisitions, this involves having not only an idea of how your target will be developed in its external markets, but also internally, which embraces the integration strategy too.

To develop an acquisition strategy you also need to understand the target's market and competitive environment in more depth – especially short- and medium-term. Often, within 12 to 24 months sudden shifts in this environment can create new trading conditions, which will either help or hamper the delivery of assumed post-acquisition performance. Here, environmental analysis does not have to be 'long-range' to highlight major threats or opportunities.

In the next subsections we look at:

- understanding our goals and present position;

- evaluating options – and search; and

- detailed evaluation.

## Understanding our goals and present position

Whilst many companies feel that that they know their own strategy and position quite well, this perception is often misplaced. Often this perception is based on some relatively basic strategy tools like SWOT analysis (strengths and weaknesses, opportunities and threats) and upon patchy data on the market and on competitors (which is mostly backward-looking and subjective feelings and impressions about the business).

Before acquisition options are explored, Fig. 6.5 gives us a useful framework through which we can understand the overall strategy for acquisitions.

This highlights a number of critical things.

- First, you must be clear about how strong your own strategic position is prior to becoming committed to a specific acquisition, or to a strategy

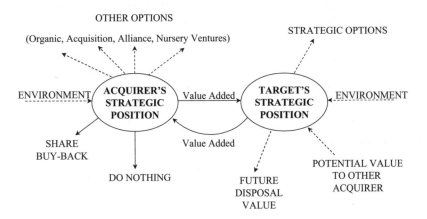

Fig. 6.5   Strategy for acquisitions.

to acquire companies generally. This includes organic development, alliances or setting up a special nursery unit for new ventures.

- Second, there may be a variety of routes to corporate development other than to acquire a particular target.

- Third, doing nothing or simply maintaining your current strategy is always an option.

- Fourth, a share buyback may actually help you to utilize surplus capital without dissipating it on ventures which destroy shareholder value.

- Fifth, value should be added by yourselves to the target (otherwise, what value do you bring to the party?) and this value should be greater than that which other acquirers would bring to this situation.

- Sixth, the target's own strategic options need to be understood fully.

- Seventh, environment changes in the external that might impact either yourself or your target need thinking through.

- Eighth, what disposal options are you likely to have should you have exhausted possibilities of adding value or be faced with better opportunities of adding value, say, in three years' time?

## Evaluating options – and search

To appraise acquisition options we again turn to the strategic option grid and the five key criteria of:

- strategic attractiveness;

- financial attractiveness;

- implementation difficulty;

- uncertainty and risk; and

- stakeholder acceptability.

This has already been well illustrated in the BMW case (see Chapter 4).

Having come up with a small list of candidates, then is the time to apply your acquisition criteria to sort out which one may be worth approaching. These criteria are best expressed as acquisition dos and don'ts, rather than as bland criteria. An example of criteria for an acquisition in the financial services industry is as follows.

- Acquisition dos:
    - we must be able to negotiate a change of name (to the group);
    - it must be of sufficient size (current profitability of over £5mn per annum) to be worth doing;
    - it must be a leader (as benchmarked by customers) in its particular niche; and
    - we must be able to keep its strong management.

- Acquisition don'ts:
    - it must not be dominated by a key individual;
    - the culture must not be too different from our own; or
    - we will not pay over £50mn for the acquisition.

These acquisition dos and don'ts take some of the emotional heat and subjectivity out of acquisition evaluation

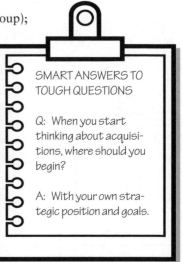

SMART ANSWERS TO TOUGH QUESTIONS

Q: When you start thinking about acquisitions, where should you begin?

A: With your own strategic position and goals.

and help inject strategic thinking into it. It is extremely helpful to do this from the point of view of dos and don'ts, which should be spelt out *prior* to any acquisition appraisal.

## Detailed evaluation

The detailed external analysis of a target focuses on understanding the inherent attractiveness of its markets – and of its competitive position. This can be achieved by using the GE grid (see Chapter 4). Ideally, you would wish your business (existing and acquisitions) to both be in inherently attractive markets and have very strong competitive positions. The GE grid is used for a number of applications relevant to acquisitions, as described below.

- First, to get a better fix on your own strategic position, as a prelude to looking at acquisitions and other options. This is split down by product/ market segment.

- Second, to analyse and evaluate the strategic position of a target acquisition, and especially to:
  - compare and contrast it vis-à-vis your own strategic position. Is there overall consistency between both business portfolios?;
  - explore whether acquisition integration can materially reposition any of these businesses, particularly in terms of relative competitive position;

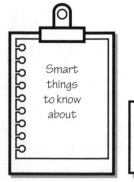

Smart
things
to know
about

---

ACQUISITIONS

Without thorough evaluation, acquisitions are like marrying someone without having gone out with them (seriously) first.

---

- understand the basis of economic profit generation in the target's business and to challenge whether this is likely to be sustainable; and
- understand how much effort in integration and investment may be required to reposition the required business in order to improve its economic profit.

## Deal-making

The deal-making process is a critical part of determining V2, which means the value added, diluted or destroyed during the negotiation. In this section the roles of acquisition options and bargaining power are explored.

Turning to the role of acquisition options and bargaining power, just which factors will actually determine V2? These can be distilled into the following five key influences.

- The strength of the acquirer's desire to buy.

- The strength of the vendor's desire to sell.

- The other options available to the acquirer – whether through alternative acquisitions, organic development or alliances.

- The other options available to the vendor – whether to dispose of the business to another party or to develop it or turn it around themselves.

- The relative time-pressure to do a deal – is it more urgent to the acquirer to do a deal or is it more urgent to the vendor?

Figure 6.6 displays this visually (along similar lines to Porter's five competitive forces (Porter 1980)) and three of these factors are examined below.

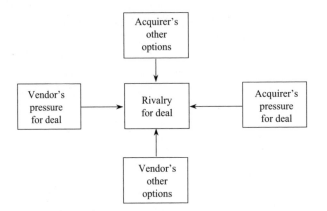

**Fig. 6.6**   Deal-making options.

### The acquirer's other options
- What options for organic development does the acquirer have?

- What alliance options does the acquirer have?

- What other acquisition options does the acquirer have?

- How attractive and flexible are these options?

### The vendor's other options
- What options exist to develop and grow the business organically – without disposal?

- What other options exist – for example, to sell to another party?

- What closure options exist for the vendor (in case of a forced sale)?

- How attractive are these alternative options?

### The time-pressure to do a deal

- What specific timetables, deadlines or other corporate pressures are driving the acquirer to want a quick deal?

- What parallel time-pressures does the vendor also face?

- Who is under most perceived time-pressure – the vendor or the acquirer?

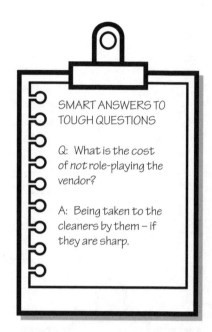

### *Integration*

The integration phase is one where value is often diluted or destroyed rather than created, and this requires further strategic thinking. This may be due to a variety of reasons, including those below.

- Integration plans may be left to emerge and, if deliberate, are inadequately thought through to deal with obstacles to change.

- There may be an abrupt change in management style, leading to lower morale and business performance, rather than improved performance.

*Smart quotes*

'Every acquisition changes the established order and pattern of activities at both firms. These changes foster uncertainty, fear, and a tendency toward self-preservation on the part of the employees. As a result, the people who are expected to create economic value for shareholders have value destroyed for themselves.'

Haspeslagh & Jemison

- Alternatively, there may be no real change in the management when one is badly needed, leading to drift (as at Rover during 1995–6).

- The acquisition period itself is a distracting time for incumbent management. There may be a period of months or longer when new developments are deferred or costs are unwisely cut. During this period the normal attention to customer delivery may be lost.

- New management might impose its own way of doing things and thus damage the acquisition's competitive strength. (At Rover Group, BMW imposed its own notion of what 'Britishness' was about, mispositioning the brand.)

- Key staff may leave, feeling (rightly or wrongly) that their career prospects are blunted.

The integration phase is important too as it is during this period when the acquirer has most opportunity to learn from the acquisition. This learning should obviously deal with the post-acquisition performance of the acquisition – financially and strategically. But it should also cover the acquisition process itself. A central question is: 'How difficult was it to integrate, and how speedily did we integrate, the acquisition relative to our expectations?'

In this next section we examine the reasons why integration strategies may fail and succeed, along with the pros and cons of different acquisition integration styles. The need to maintain business continuity is then addressed. This leads on to the need to project manage integration and the associated organizational issues. The need to monitor and learn from performance is then highlighted, as are the links to post-acquisition learning and review.

## Why integration may succeed or fail

Acquisition integration can fail for a large number of reasons. Figure 6.7 captures these reasons as a fishbone analysis. Using the fishbone, the key symptom of the problem is shown at the right-hand side of the page – at the fish's 'head'. The underlying root causes of the problem are depicted as the bones of the fishbone. (Note there is no special order to the fishbone analysis display.)

Figure 6.7 highlights some of the main reasons for failure. These range from there not being an effective and robust strategy in the very first place through to inadequate integration planning and project management and inappropriate organizational change. Typically, unsuccessful integration processes are characterized by a lack of decisiveness on the part of the acquiring management team or through inappropriate and damaging interventions.

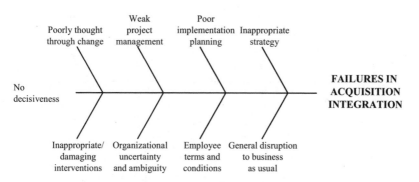

**Fig. 6.7**  Fishbone analysis in failures in acquisition integration.

It is useful to examine (at a more positive level) what factors would need to line up to deliver a particularly effective implementation process. This is depicted in Fig. 6.8 (wishbone analysis). Notice that while some of these alignment factors are reversals of the fishbone analysis, some of them are not, and all of them are not in any way average, but more superior or visionary.

*Integration strategies – the pros and cons*

Integration strategies can range along a continuum, from:

- leave alone;

- to putting managers in to complement; and

- to installing a new management team.

There are obviously choices too as to the speed of the intervention. Changes can be implemented immediately, or after a period of, say, six to nine

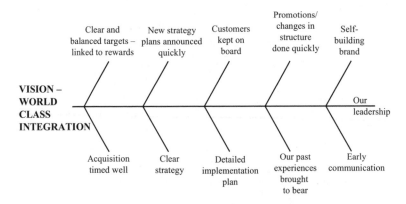

Fig. 6.8   Wishbone analysis of successes in acquisition integration.

months, or perhaps after around eighteen months. Whilst there can be no hard and fast rules of how to approach these changes, the following recipes are well worth remembering.

- If you think you are going to need to make changes, do this as soon as possible – do not procrastinate.

- The decision as to what extent you do need to make changes depends very much on:
  - current management's strengths and weaknesses;
  - flexibility (or lack of it) in the current management's mindset; and
  - the requirements of the future business strategy and its associated competitive challenges.

- The value which you feel you can add to the acquisition, and your own team's existing competencies.

- The amount of available management skills that you have and the opportunity cost of deploying them on this particular acquisition.

- Unless integration is managed well, organizational morale can easily go into a downward spiral. This can be represented in Fig. 6.9, where morale over time is plotted against organizational performance over time.

- Ironically, whilst acquisitions are made ostensibly in order to generate increased performance, in the short run this performance typically declines – due to organizational fear. Where an experienced acquirer is involved, the opposite effect is frequently created: the integration situation gives management a new clarity and sense of challenge. The integration strategy of conglomerate Hanson plc was very much along these lines: there, newly promoted middle managers had a real appetite for delivery results, freed from the limiting mindset of previous senior managers.

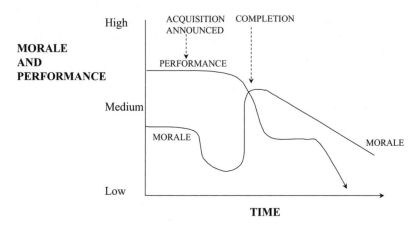

**Fig. 6.9** Organizational morale.

*Acquisition learning checklists*

- The integration projects – were these as attractive and as easy as was assumed?

- Were interdependencies managed as well as they needed to be?

- Did new, external brakes on performance crystallize, and what was their impact?

- Were internal performance drivers managed as well as was hoped for, and did new internal brakes on performance materialize?

- Why did specific performance problems occur? (Fishbone analysis.)

- Were all the critical assumptions about the whole acquisition integration identified, and did we understand their importance/degree of uncertainty?

- What are customer or staff perceptions of the appropriateness of integration strategies or tactics and are these perceptions adverse or have they deteriorated, and if so, why was this? (Fishbone analysis.)

More specifically (and based on lessons from similar reviews of acquisition integration elsewhere), the following key questions can home in on some likely generic areas of difficulty or blockage.

- Was the brand strategy (post-integration) appropriate?

- Was the quality of the target's management as good as we thought?

- Did the changes to key individuals in the management team work, and well, and if not, why not?

- Did we really understand pending competitive shifts in the environment?

- Were our assumptions about life-cycle effects impacting on the acquisition's product range – and also on their competition strengths and weaknesses – valid?

- Were assumed investment levels to deliver V3 adequate or not?

- Did we lose key personnel by mishandling the softer issues (for example, restructuring, management development, remuneration, perks, etc.)?

- Did we intervene inappropriately in operational practices – causing unnecessary disruption?

- Were we really clever in defining our integration strategy and integration projects or did these change considerably in scope and difficulty over the first 18 months?

- Did we devote enough time and attention to managing the acquisition integration?

- Finally, what lessons can we draw from this for integrating any future acquisitions?

## Granada versus Forte – a case study

### Background

Forte, a leisure conglomerate, fell prey to Granada plc in 1996. Granada made a convincing case to Forte's shareholders that they could add more value to the Forte portfolio through the disposal of some businesses and through post-acquisition integration.

In 1995 Forte's turnover stood at £1789mn (with net profits before tax of £127mn). In 1995 Granada had overtaken Forte with an impressive operating profit of £388mn, with operations principally in the UK. Forte, by contrast, had extensive international operations – it had hotels in North America, the Caribbean, South America, Africa, the Middle and Far East, Australasia, Europe and Moscow. Forte's major hotel brands included:

- exclusive hotels (18 hotels, 3600 rooms);

- Forte Meridian (85 hotels, 23,400 rooms);

- Forte Posthouse (80 hotels, 10,000 rooms);

- Forte Heritage (52 hotels, 2600 rooms); and

- other hotels (12 hotels, 6200 rooms).

(Source: *Forte Defence Document*, 1995)

This case study is set out as follows:

- Forte's current strategic and financial position;

- Granada's turnaround and strategic intent;

- the Granada bid;

- Forte's defence; and

- Granada's first year of integration.

## Forte's current strategic and financial position

Forte's 1995 Annual Report and Accounts began with a confident statement from its chairman Sir Rocco Forte:

*'We have embarked on a strategy of building powerful hotel and restaurant brands through effective marketing, focused geographical expansion, innovative product development and a high customer service orientation amongst our people.'*

Reading this statement, one might be forgiven for wondering *how* Forte became so vulnerable. Profit before tax in the year ending 1995 was £127mn, 65% up on the previous year. Earnings per share were up 80%. But Forte

Group's past track record was not so impressive. Table 6.1 shows highlights from the previous five years.

**Table 6.1** Forte plc summary results 1991–5; figures in £mn.

|  | 1995 | 1994 | 1993 | 1992 | 1991 |
|---|---|---|---|---|---|
| Sales | 1,789 | 2,106 | 2,721 | 2,662 | 2,641 |
| Net profit | 258 | 225 | 227 | 204 | 289 |
| Net interest | (131) | (148) | (167) | (143) | (111) |
|  | 127 | 77 | 60 | 61 | 178 |
| Profits on disposals less losses | — | 34 | 93 | (17) | (2) |
| Profit after interest, before tax (1) | 127 | 111 | 153 | 44 | 176 |
| Total net assets (2) | 2,464 | 2,352 | 2,718 | 3,020 | 3,052 |
| Return on net assets (1) ÷ (2) (weighted average = 4.5%) | 5.1% | 4.7% | 5.6% | 1.4% | 5.7% |

Forte had gone through a period of strategic drift, followed by a turnaround strategy which was only partly realized. But although a recovery in earnings was underway (by shedding its less profitable turnover) the question was: was this recovery being pushed as quickly and as effectively as was possible? Could the value of Forte's portfolio be released either by more effective management or by selling the business on to another parent? But clearly the historical performance (up to 1995) might not reflect the underlying value of the business – both in terms of potential cash-streams and asset value. Forte was undervalued – and this was spotted by Granada's management.

Forte's hotels operated in 60 countries with 940 hotels (with 97,000 rooms) and 600 restaurants. They included more exclusive hotels, like Meridian and the Savoy, and the more lower/middle-market Forte Posthouse and 115 budget Travelodges. The restaurant business included the Little Chef and

Happy Eater chains, which dominate the British roadside, and the motor-way service stations, Welcome Break.

Forte thus presented itself as a relatively diverse group with a variety of generic marketing strategies within its portfolio, including:

- a differentiated/niche strategy (at Savoy/Meridian);

- a cost leadership/broad strategy (at Little Chef); and

- a cost leadership/niche strategy (at Travelodge).

The operating profits of Forte's businesses break down as in Table 6.2.

Table 6.2   Forte operating profits; figures in £mn.

|  | 1995 | 1994 |
| --- | --- | --- |
| Hotels | 175 | 136 |
| Restaurants | 82 | 67 |
|  | 257 | 203 |

The hotel businesses' turnover and operating profits were as in Tables 6.3 and 6.4.

Table 6.3   Forte sales – hotels only; figures in £mn.

|  | 1995 | 1994 |
| --- | --- | --- |
| London | 232 | 204 |
| Other UK | 421 | 401 |
| Total UK | 653 | 605 |
| International | 359 | 337 |
|  | 1012 | 942 |

**Table 6.4** Forte operating profits – hotels only; figures in £mn.

|  | 1995 | 1994 |
|---|---|---|
| London | 69 | 53 |
| Other UK | 81 | 70 |
| Total UK | 150 | 123 |
| International | 26 | 13 |
|  | 176 | 136 |

These profit improvements were due to improvements in volumes (occupancy up by 6%), but average rates only increased by 2%, indicating price rises just under the level of inflation. Meanwhile, the restaurant businesses' results were as in Tables 6.5 and 6.6.

**Table 6.5** Forte sales – restaurants only; figures in £mn.

|  | 1995 | 1994 |
|---|---|---|
| UK | 584 | 558 |
| Europe | 70 | 64 |
|  | 654 | 622 |

**Table 6.6** Forte operating profits – restaurants only; figures in £mn.

|  | 1995 | 1994 |
|---|---|---|
| UK | 74 | 60 |
| Europe | 8 | 7 |
|  | 82 | 67 |

These improvements were partly due to improved margins of 12.5% (from 11%) and higher-than-average spending in roadside restaurants.

In summary, prior to Granada's bid, Forte had achieved a good deal to effect a short-term turnaround. Whether it had done enough is another question, because its financial performance was still less than satisfactory from a shareholder value point of view.

*Granada's acquisition strategy (and portfolio)*

In earlier times Granada was run by the Bernstein family in what has been described as a 'paternalistic' way. When its new chief executive Gerald Robinson joined Granada, profits had fallen to £56.9mn. On the Wednesday of Granada's initial bid, profits stood at £351mn on turnover of £2.38bn. This turnaround had made him extremely popular in the City. According to one institutional source, some watchers in the City believe that 'he [Robinson] walks on water'. Granada had acquired Sutcliffe Catering and London Weekend Television and had produced major profit improvements there. This resulted in a wide spread of activities, as follows:

- broadcasting and production (LWT and Granada);

- other leisure (Granada, night clubs, studio tours);

- computer services;

- TV rental;

- motorway services (Granada, Pavilion, Burger Express);

- hotels (and lodges);

- theme parks;

- workplace services;

- contract catering (Sutcliffe);

- travel; and

- investments (BSkyB, ITN).

## Granada's bid

According to *The Sunday Times* (26 November 1995), Sir Rocco Forte, chairman of Forte, could not believe the rumours that Forte was shortly to be in play as a bid target. Disbelieving these stories, he chose not to alter his plans for a pheasant shoot in Yorkshire. Apparently, he was still shaving at 8 a.m. when he heard that Granada had mounted a hostile £3.3bn bid for the group.

Ironically, just three months previously, Sir Rocco had played golf with Gerry Robinson, Granada's chief executive, who had (perhaps unsurprisingly) not even as much as hinted at an interest in the group. This particular bid was especially surprising to Forte because it seemed to them implausible that Granada had the skills to run a complex international group like Forte.

The £3.3bn bid by Granada valued Forte shares at 328p, thus valuing Forte at 25 times its (then) current earnings. This represented a 19% premium to Forte's pre-bid share price. Immediately, Forte's shares soared 71p to 346p, 18p over Granada's initial offer price. First impressions in financial markets were therefore that 'Forte's independence is doomed' and that Granada would bid more.

Forte's own projections of Granada's post-acquisition gearing estimated this as being over 200% (up from 50% prior to the acquisition), and that debt would soar to over £3.1bn (Source: *Forte Defence Document*, 1995). This raised the question: 'Would Granada become a highly-geared, forced seller of assets at distressed prices?' (and thus having a negative V1). Granada felt this level of gearing would be both temporary and manageable. Forte's view was that Granada would find it extremely tough to recoup value.

A major institutional shareholder, Mercury Asset Management (MAM), held a substantial stake in both companies: 12.5% in Forte and 14.8% in Granada. So how MAM chose to play its cards was a key factor influencing the outcome of Granada's hostile bid. Further, Sir Rocco Forte, who was both chairman and chief executive of Forte, may have not have spent enough time communicating with his key institutional shareholders as perhaps he might have.

Questions that investors like MAM needed to ask themselves in order to be persuaded to back the Granada bid were as follows.

- Was Robinson's Granada the best qualified management to rejuvenate Forte's brand names? *The Financial Times* (7 December 1995) asked: 'Was Granada management such a magic quality that it could work well in different industries?'

- Did the Granada move hark back to the period of macho deal-making associated with the, by now, unfashionable period of the conglomerate?

- Was Granada's progress on the earnings front at least partially due to a number of large restructuring provisions following past acquisitions? And was Robinson's record for improving the performance of acquired companies actually based on sound, longer-term strategic development?

- Would the highly cash-generative television business of Granada face cashflow dilution from the more capital-hungry, low-cash-yield and cyclical business of hotels?

- Were Granada's finances sufficiently strong to support a bid on this scale?

- Granada's own net worth of a mere £585mn appeared small against Forte's net assets of £2.5bn. Granada would need to borrow around £1.5bn. If one combined the net assets of the businesses following the acquisition, these would shrink from £3bn to £1.6bn (figures per *The Financial Times*, 7 December 1995), whilst combined borrowings would rise from £1.9bn to £3.3bn. This produced a gearing of 213% (which is £3.3bn divided by £1.9bn, multiplied by 100).

By late December 1995 Forte moved remarkably fast to repel Granada. Particularly given the timescales in which it had responded, its bid defence was an impressive feat. Sir Rocco had put forward an apparently credible number of measures, including:

- a plan to sell its restaurant business and the Travelodge chain of budget hotels to Whitbread for over £1bn;

- a revaluation of its hotels to £3.1bn (10% above its estimated value in January 1994); and

- an increase in its dividend, which was cut to 7.5p from 9.9p in January 1993 (this dividend was last raised five years previously).

The proposed disposal to Whitbread included 364 Little Chef and 68 Happy Easter roadside restaurants, 30 French and 30 British service stations, and 127 Travelodge hotels. This deal, in effect, increased the pressure on Granada to raise its bid. From Forte's point of view these disposals would have virtually wiped out Forte's £1.2bn debt (including leasebacks), assuming no repayment of shareholders' capital.

In effect, Forte, by unbundling its own business portfolio, sought to outdo Granada in unlocking the value trapped inside the group and to do part of Granada's integration and rationalization strategy itself. But the real question was: could Forte do a more effective job in generating synergistic value, sweat value and value created by improving and developing competitive position?

But Forte's defence document also disclosed damaging facts: its top hotels accounted for *one-third* of total assets but contributed just over *14%* of operating profits.

## Granada's first year in charge

On 9 January 1996, Granada then increased its offer for Forte from £3.24bn to £3.74bn, presenting this revised bid as a 'knockout blow' *(The Financial Times*, January 1996). Granada also announced the early sale of Forte's Meridian hotels (assuming their bid was successful). Granada's bid of £3.74bn was still some margin below Robinson's 'walk-away-from price' at which Granada would have been indifferent as to whether the bid went ahead or not.

Granada's average cost savings in the first year were estimated at £100mn. The cost savings included the (inevitable) closure of Forte's London head-quarters and the sale of the Forte corporate jet. Ironically, Granada took Forte's own figures of £24mn of cost savings and then simply added a better way of doing this. Also, several months after the actual deal, press comment appeared to the effect that there was no sign of Granada selling the corporate jet. Besides these areas of performance improvement, Granada also assumed a saving of 5% of purchasing costs. Indeed, in the first year following completion, Granada: (a) exceeded its profit targets for the remaining Forte businesses; and (b) was on schedule with most of its property disposals of the top-market hotels.

Granada thus seemed to have opted for a mass-market focus with selectively higher prices and lower costs. Forte had opted for a spread of operations across the spectrum of the hotel industry – and with an enormous span of market positioning.

Granada proposed to retain (and improve):

- Forte Posthouse;

- Forte Travelodge;

- Little Chef;

- Happy Eater; and

- Côte France.

(*The Financial Times*, 10 January 1996.)

Granada intended to sell both Forte's Exclusive chain of hotels and the Meridian chain. Surprisingly, after the acquisition, Granada decided to keep the Meridian (*The Times*, 23 May 1996). This apparently surprised City analysts, and also Sir Rocco, who had been hoping to buy both the Exclusive and the Meridian chains. (Indeed, by 1999 the Meridian had become a strong, growing brand, particularly in the US, and was showing a very healthy profit stream.)

Granada adopted a piecemeal disposal strategy for the Exclusive hotels. Although it achieved a good price for the Hyde Park Hotel (£86mn – £16mn over book value), by late 1996 it became apparent that other properties would be much harder to sell at good prices. (*The Times,* November 1996, described the Exclusive portfolio as a 'mixed one'.)

Granada's initial integration strategy was thus to:

- achieve a quantum improvement in Forte's marketing and cost controls (especially of overheads and through purchasing economies);

- dispose of Forte's 68% stake in the Savoy Hotel Group;

- dispose of Forte's motorway service stations, Lillywhites (sporting groups) and other minor businesses;

- rejuvenate the restaurant businesses, with better pricing and positioning (especially at the Little Chef and Happy Eater chains);

- increase prices at Posthouse and Travelodge chains by 20–25%; and

- achieve significant purchasing economies.

By late 1996, Granada had moved fast to integrate Forte's businesses. This included:

- cost-cutting at head office;

- price rises in the Travelodge chain and testing out of Travelodge city centre sites;

- new menus at both Little Chef and Happy Eater (apparently adding Burger King outlets has doubled average turnover – *The Times*, 7 October 1996);

- the planned sale of the Exclusive hotels for around £850mn;

- a new management team was put into Meridian to manage the hotels as a group rather than individually; and

- extensions were planned to Posthouse hotels, to increase turnover.

Granada had certainly moved very fast to harvest the value potential of V3 (especially by generating 'sweat value'), and in 1997 more disposals were made. Robinson also announced plans to introduce Burger King outlets into at least 100 Little Chefs (to increase their youth appeal). This, apparently, proved to be a very successful move – with large increases in turnover being achieved.

With a rapid rate of disposal and assuming a healthy free cashflow from combined business, debt was projected as falling to a more comfortable level by September 1997 from its peak at £3.7bn just after the acquisition. This reduced gearing to just 70%, based on existing asset valuations. So, Granada proved that it had not only avoided overpaying for Forte but it had also hoped to demonstrate that (without artificial financial engineering) it could genuinely deliver shareholder value through its investment in Forte.

## Key lessons from Granada and Forte

A number of key lessons can be drawn out of this case study on acquisition strategy and integration. These include the following.

- A question mark hangs over Granada's motives in acquiring Forte. Granada's bid was only just timed right, as Forte was on a recovery path, and Granada had to pay in excess of 25 times the (recently improved) earnings for its businesses. A detached observer might well conclude that Granada's new business portfolio was *almost* as complex as the original

Forte one. There is an argument here that we may have merely seen one corporate conglomerate replaced by another.

- Forte's bid defence reflected a degree of astuteness which appears to have taken Granada aback. Forte made considerable capital out of the strategic attractiveness of its business, which any potential investor could do in order to get a really good price (or in this case, to claim that existing management could do a better job). Did Granada really think through Forte's countermoves (and how they would respond to them)? This highlights the need to work out in some depth the deal negotiation strategy and tactics.

- Further, Granada's integration strategies for the rump of Forte's businesses were certainly radical, but were they sufficiently well thought through? In the press comment, the main focus was on the corporate wrestling match rather than on how the 'winner' would be able to cash in on his assumed trophy.

We can now summarize the acquisition logic by going back to our acquisition values – V1, V2 and V3 (see Table 6.7).

Acquisitions are thus a dangerous terrain, both financially and strategically. On the surface, acquisitions are primarily an issue of deal-making and fi-

Table 6.7   Granada and Forte – a summary of acquisition values.

| Sources of V1 | Sources of V2 | Sources of V3 |
| --- | --- | --- |
| Hotels business – markets were growing, margins improving again | Sell off up-market hotels | Marketing improvement and innovation |
| Roadside restaurants had strong positions in relatively attractive markets | Find ready buyers for some roadside restaurants | Cost-cutting and synergy management |
| Improvements by Forte management now coming through | Granada's deal-making skills | Granada's integration skills |

nancial engineering. Whilst these activities are clearly central, of themselves they may not provide the complete recipe for adding shareholder value. Effective integration is also needed. In addition, managers need to do sufficient strategic thinking to anticipate where to add value post-acquisition, and also how they will achieve this during integration. Granada, on balance, appears to have been successful in this process and (as at early 2000) contemplated huge major media acquisitions, with its market capitalization standing at around an impressive £11bn.

The main integration successes of Granada can be summed up as follows.

- Granada's pre-acquisition integration strategy was substantially carried out – and successfully.

- Where Granada changed this strategy, it actually enhanced shareholder value – for example, in the retention and development of Meridian hotels.

- Granada's cost savings efforts were mainly successful.

- Granada did manage to squeeze more margins out of its new businesses.

- A new culture and mindset was brought into the Forte organization.

Acquisition integration was not, however, an unqualified success. For example, the following drawbacks arose.

- Some of the hotel disposals took longer than had been anticipated.

- When prices at Travelodges were increased by around 15%, turnover fell off in volume terms – and quite considerably.

- In order to increase margins at the Little Chef roadside cafés, new menus were brought out. These confused both staff and customers alike. Over the first nine months, no less than two different sets of new menu were in use.

- Granada decided to outsource certain operations in order to realize profits. At its Posthouse hotels it was forced to revert to in-sourcing some of these activities as a result of new suppliers being unable to meet the required service levels.

- Some of its refurbishment of certain hotels was not thought through, resulting in this needing to be redone only 18 months later.

---

ACQUISITIONS

1 The value of an acquisition comes from:
- V1 – the internal value of the business, given its strategic position;
- V2 – the value created or destroyed during the deal; and
- V3 – the value created or destroyed during integration.

2 V1 depends on the growth drivers, the five competitive forces and the company's own competitive position.

3 Acquisition can generate protective value, opportunity value, synergistic value or sweat value.

4 Acquisitions demand a robust process – to avoid the thrill of the chase.

5 Anything other than a deliberate strategy for an acquisition is very dangerous.

6 You should begin by looking at your own strategic position (and goals).

7 Use the strategic option grid to evaluate the options.

8 You need to specify (in advance) more detailed criteria (and dos and don'ts).

9 Use the GE grid to assess underlying strategic attractiveness.

10 V2 is determined by: (a) the bargaining context around the deal: and (b) your bargaining process and skills.

11 Integration needs further strategic thinking, great clarity and skilful implementation.

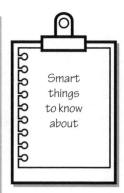

Smart things to know about

# 7

# Implementing Growth Strategies

'That's the problem. Just about everybody agrees on what management is. "The art of and science of directing effort and resources so that the established objectives of an enterprise may be attained in accordance with accepted policies" is one definition. It is the "How" that nobody is quite sure about.'

'Pooh nodded, assuming his wise-bear look. "How is difficult," he said. "If you ask Eeyore how he is, he almost always says, "not very how." Everyone has trouble with "How".'

A.A. Milne, *Winnie the Pooh*

### Introduction – the 'Kama Sutra' approach to implementation

Throughout the book we stress the importance of being obsessive about creating options. Whilst there are invariably more than a number of options for *what* to grow, there are actually even more for *how* to grow. This can be likened to that most famous book on human leisure pastimes – the *Kama Sutra*. For just as in that domain there may be a hundred ways to implement that particular strategy, so for growth strategies there are likely to be equally many.

In this important chapter on implementation we take you through a step-by-step process implemented (in part or in whole) by Nokia, Royal Bank of Scotland, Tesco and many other successful growth companies. We take you through scoping the implementation with, 'from-to' analysis, more advanced fishbone analysis, and through project scoping. In the next phase of the process we examine implementation difficulty and stakeholder support.

## Scoping implementation – with 'from-to' (FT) analysis

'From-to' (FT) analysis helps to scope the extent of the growth project on which you are working, but in terms of its breadth and its degree of stretch. FT analysis is another useful tool for scoping the extent of implementation, especially for organizational change or operational development. Where a growth project has a significant impact on 'how we do things around here'

*Smart quotes*

'No company can escape the need to reskill its people, reshape its product portfolio, redesign its processes, and redirect resources. Organizational transformation is an imperative for every enterprise. The real issue is whether transformation happens belatedly – in a crisis atmosphere – or with foresight – in a calm and considered atmosphere; whether the transformation agenda is set by more prescient competitors or derives from one's own point of view about the future; whether transformation is spasmodic and brutal or continuous and peaceful.'

Hamel & Prahalad

or the 'paradigm' (see Grundy, 1993), then it is essential that at least a rudimentary FT analysis is conducted.

For example, managers within the Prudential insurance company performed an FT analysis for their infrastructure for growth, as shown in Table 7.1.

This kind of analysis can also be used to monitor the progress of a growth project, perhaps using a score of 1 to 5, with 1 being the 'from' and 5 being the possible 'to'. In some situations, however, we might well be starting off with better than a 1, as we might already have made some progress towards our goals, prior to embarking on the project. Equally, we might wish to go all out for a 5, as a 4 or even 3 might be more realistic and acceptable, depending upon the situation.

**Table 7.1**  Prudential FT analysis.

| PARADIGM | FROM | TO |
|---|---|---|
| POWER | Restricted | Resides at the lowest appropriate level |
| STRUCTURE | Hierarchical | Flatter |
| CONTROLS | Instinctive and 'seat of pants' | Measured objectives |
| ROUTINES | Retrospective | Live and forward-looking |
| RITUALS | Loose plans | Structured plans |
| MYTHS | The 'Mighty Pru' | Real world – 'life administration is OK' |
| STORIES | Our job well done | Delighted customers |
| SYMBOLS | Status hierarchy | Rewards for performance |
| MANAGEMENT STYLE | Aloof | Open |

The Prudential example of FT analysis is very much a more 'gourmet' approach. We see a semi-structured approach being used to generate the key shifts that the growth project is aimed at delivering. A simplified approach is to quickly brainstorm the 'froms' and 'tos' in a way much more specific to a particular growth project. Our main caveat here is that you really must think about the softer factors which are required to shift: for example, behaviours, attitudes and mindset generally.

To perform an FT analysis, you need to answer the following questions.

- What are you trying to shift (either externally or internally – the critical categories)?

- By how much are you trying to shift them (the horizontal 'from' and 'to' shifts)?

FT analysis is particularly useful for comparing and contrasting either past and future growth drivers or the competitive forces. By now, it may have become apparent to you that FT analysis is essentially an extended form of gap analysis (see our previous section). Because it breaks down the gap into a number of dimensions, it is generally more specific than gap analysis and is frequently the next step on.

*Exercise – FT analysis*

For one area of growth of your choice and, in particular, one for which there is already an existing state of affairs that you are trying to change or shift, ask the following.

- What are the key dimensions that you are trying to shift?

FT ANALYSIS

- It gives a clear and more complete vision of the extent of, and the potential difficulty, that achieving the growth strategy may give rise to.
- It can be used to actually monitor strategic progress.
- It is a very useful technique for communicating what needs to be done or for exploring the implications and for getting greater buy-in.
- More specifically, it is especially helpful in presenting business plans.

- What are the extremes of these shifts (from left to right) – i.e. where have you started from originally and where would you like to end up ultimately?

- Where actually are you now? (Note: this does not have to be a 1.)

- Where do you want to be as a result of this growth project? (Note: this does not have to be a 5.)

- What specific actions or interventions might make each shift feasible?

## Advanced issue diagnosis – with 'piranha' analysis

Fishbone analysis can be of considerable help in structuring problems. Generally, several problems hide inside each other but are interrelated. This invites splitting them out in a way where they are still linked. We call this 'piranha' analysis, to highlight the fact that whilst smaller problems can appear to be more manageable, they can be actually deadly and ferocious (hence the piranha analogy).

Figure 7.1 gives an excellent example of this, using a relationship problem as its focus. Relationship problems are endemic in complex, changing organ-

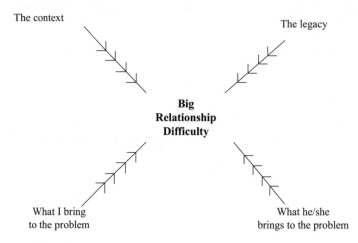

The context                                          The legacy

**Big Relationship Difficulty**

What I bring                                 What he/she
to the problem                            brings to the problem

**Fig. 7.1**    Piranha analysis.

izations (not to mention in personal lives), and strategic thinking is a vital tool in helping you deal with them. Typical relationship difficulties occur with your boss, with a subordinate or with a close rival. Figure 7.1 splits into four piranha problem areas:

- what you bring to it yourself;

- what others bring to it;

- the current organizational context; and

- the past organizational legacy.

This problem structure forces you into assessing what you brought to the situation. Besides helping you become more objective, it also focuses on something over which you ought to have much more influence – yourself!

The 'context' should generate some thinking about what is currently going on around the relationship – for example, restructuring, performance pressures, inconsistent organizational priorities. The 'legacy' can, in some situations, be very important as it helps to understand how the problem might have developed and how this might have been at least partially caused by past organizational mistakes.

## How-how analysis – project scoping

How-how analysis is useful in the detailed planning of implementation. It is also useful in finding a way forward which might not have been thought about before. Figure 7.2 gives an example of a how-how analysis, where, until this picture was drawn up, managers perceived that there was no way that the cost of bought-in motors could be reduced.

While fishbone analysis works backwards from the current situation to find out how and why it exists, how-how analysis works forwards to see how it

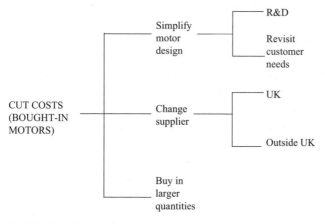

**Fig. 7.2** How-how analysis.

can be resolved in the future. How-how analysis adds the most value when you have not really thought very hard about the detailed implementation steps that will be needed to achieve something. But even when you have thought about this, it will also be useful just to help identify the less tangible as well as the tangible aspects of implementation, especially:

- positioning;

- communicating;

- influencing; and

- team-building.

How-how analysis will also help to get some approximate order of the likely sequence in which things need to happen – and potential critical paths. How-how's major benefits are that it is common sense and it exposes assumptions about what actually has to happen, thereby reducing blind-spots.

How-how analysis works by starting off with the core growth task, such as to enter a new market (see Fig. 7.2). This begins at the left-hand side of the page. By working from left to right, one repeatedly asks the question: 'How is that particular task to be achieved?' This produces more and more detail until a complete listing of activities is created. Whilst at this stage these activities are not phased over time, this should give a really detailed idea of project activities.

With how-how analysis, it is crucial to expand the activities to those softer areas which may also be required to achieve the required result. This might entail training or other support for behavioural or mindset change. Once the major activities have been generated, the next stage is to begin to think about their phasing over time. This can be done in either of two ways:

- with a project with relatively few interdependencies in the sequencing of activities, one can go directly to a Gantt chart, which displays activities over particular times; or

- with a project where there are likely to be extensive interdependencies in the sequencing of activities, one might seek instead to develop the 'activity network'.

A Gantt chart (named after its creator) is shown in Fig. 7.3 – for the business turnaround underlying the network of opportunities, it may still be worthwhile doing a quick Gantt chart to get a 'feel' for when things may need to happen by.

Once again, we should not see Gantt analysis as a mechanistic process, for there are frequently many possible phasings of these activities. Even where

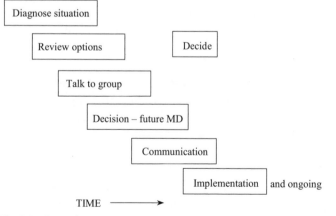

Fig. 7.3   Gantt chart.

there are well-trodden ways of doing particular kinds of projects – such as clinical research projects in the pharmaceutical industry – there are still often choices as to when activities can begin, and in what order they happen.

Managing growth through project management is a way of increasing time-based competitive advantage (Stalk, 1990). In most industries it is becoming increasingly important to accelerate the implementation of business growth. For example, with the advance of Internet-based marketing, many companies are in danger of being left behind in the race to revolutionize communication with, and transactions between, buyers electronically. Here, being six months late to market may well mean the difference between spectacular success and abject failure. As such, it is crucial to parallel-work as many activities as is practical in order to accelerate implementation.

To illustrate, one senior Tesco manager once said to me: 'What we are trying to achieve in two weeks, Tony, is what we and others used to achieve in three to six months.' Growth projects, as we have already defined them, are all about achieving a pre-targeted result in a specific time and at a specific cost. It is therefore imperative to see what we can do (through Gantt chart analysis, and through the activity network and the critical path) to accelerate these.

A very solid rule of thumb which might help us to achieve this is: try to do activities sooner than you might otherwise think of doing. This rule of thumb applies especially to activities which are more likely to be on the critical path, and those which are most constraining.

Besides parallel-working activities and accelerating the start of activities, it is also perhaps possible to split the activity up into at least two phases. The most obvious phases are planning and implementation. For example, even if you cannot do an activity now, you can certainly create a *plan* for it.

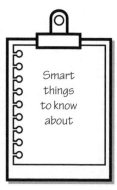

## Force-field analysis

Force-field analysis is a technique which brings to the surface the underlying forces which may pull a particular change forward or which may prevent progress, or even move the change backwards. These forces can be separately identified as 'enablers' or 'constraints', but neither set of forces can be adequately identified without first specifying the objectives of the implementation.

When managers first see force-field analysis they often read it as being some form of extended cost-benefit or 'pros-and-cons' analysis, which it is definitely not. Force-field analysis is simply concerned with the difficulty of the journey which a strategy is likely to make throughout its implementation. The difficulty of this journey, like that of any other journey in life, has nothing to do with the attractiveness of reaching the destination. The only sense in which it is permissible to incorporate the perceived benefits of a strategy as a force-field enabler is insofar as there is actually a genuinely attractive business case for the strategy and one which has turned on key stakeholders, and/or that key stakeholders are attracted by the strategy for other reasons.

*Smart quotes*

'Just often it is like marshmallows. Sometimes you have got a group of people around the table like marshmallows. If you push them in they kind of blob out again. They blob about like marshmallows – it is marshmallow theory. If you hold them over the fire though you get a kind of chemical reaction.'

Karen Slatford, Hewlett-Packard

The most effective way of evaluating the forces enabling or constraining achievement of the strategy's objective is to do so pictorially. This picture represents the relative strength of each individual enabling or constraining force by drawing an arrowed line whose length is in proportion to that relative strength.

A horizontal version of force-field analysis is depicted in Fig. 7.4. Note in this case that, on balance, the enabling forces appear less strong than the constraining forces. This particular analysis is for a telecommunication company's strategic plan. It shows that, although many of the plans, processes and programmes had been put in place, it was nevertheless difficult to envisage implementation being a complete success. Subsequent events suggested that implementation difficulties at the company were very severe.

The example of the telecommunications company highlights one important truth about force-field analysis, namely that the degree of ease of the growth strategy is only in proportion to the extent of your pre-existing *cunning*

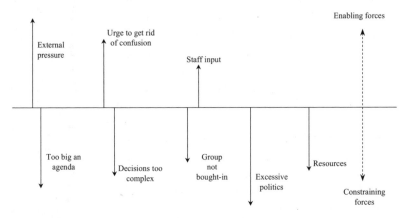

Fig. 7.4   Force-field analysis – telecommunications company.

FORCE-FIELD ANALYSIS

Anticipate the difficulty of:

- a growth strategy;
- achieving your objectives;
- developing your own capability;
- getting a different job; and
- actually doing it.

*implementation plan.* Managers who have not already thought hard about the phases of difficulty and about options to get around potential hurdles (for example, 'push' versus 'pull' strategies) for the growth strategy may be doomed to suffer a Very Difficult Project.

As a rule of thumb, one would wish to see the enablers outweighing the constraints by a factor of at least 1.5 to 2 overall, in accordance with the principle of military dominance. Otherwise we should be concerned and potentially worried that implementation droop will set in. Also, any stoppers really must be addressed, otherwise implementation won't happen. During (and before) implementation, the key implementation forces should be continually monitored to ensure that none threatens to 'go critical' and become a stopper.

*Smart quotes*

'Strategic thinking can be frustrated by the team. In some cases the pace of change is going really fast. And some people say "and this too will pass – we will drag it out as long as we can and it will have changed by the time we have to get to the end of it and have to implement it. Oh my God, this is too painful, how can I make this not happen to me".'

Karen Slatford, Hewlett-Packard

The next issue that arises is how to evaluate the relative strength of the various forces. Two methods used successfully in the past include:

- scoring each force as having high, medium or low impact; and

- scoring each force numerically on a scale of 1 to 5.

Where a team may wish to change its mind (and does not wish to spoil its artwork), then by using Post-It notes the length of the arrows can be changed. Most groups of managers work comfortably by using the high/medium/low scoring method. In exceptional cases (for example, where managers have scientific backgrounds or have an inherent love of quantification) the numerical 1 to 5 scale appears to fit more comfortably.

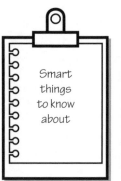

FORCE-FIELD ANALYSIS

- It encourages you to think about difficulty, as opposed merely to attractiveness.
- It helps you to focus on the context and process for implementation, rather than its context.
- It gives an early warning of Mission Impossible projects.

## Difficulty-over-time curves

Whilst force-field analysis is very good at tackling short- and medium-term difficulty, it may not stretch managers' thinking about the longer-term dynamics of implementation. To address this issue we need the 'difficulty-over-time' curve (see Fig. 7.5).

This plots the precise degree of difficulty (easy, difficult or very difficult) over time.

'But the key figure at the top should have a kind of evangelical fanaticism about what the strategy is. Unless you have this, you are not going to manage to convince people. For example, last year I called our plans "going from good to great". And we didn't go from good to great, we got better. So I said "This is good to great part II". We could be back here next year doing part III or even part IV, but one day we will get there and I ain't leaving here until we do.'

Lord Thurso, MD of Champneys

Sometimes implementation gets easier over time, but more commonly it gets more difficult. This can occur at all kinds of different stages – perhaps as a steady incline or, alternatively, difficulty could climb a little, then fall back before getting really, really difficult.

This reminds the author of his experience on a rollercoaster in Los Angeles. It appeared to be two rollercoasters, one small and one which was quite awesome. He thought he had gone on the small one until he went over the

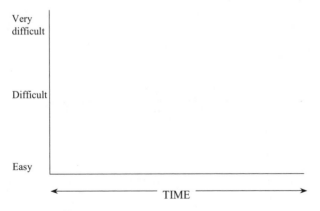

**Fig. 7.5**  Difficulty-over-time curve.

first peak to see the Very Big One right ahead. The experience was amplified by the fact that it was very quiet and early in the day. Indeed, he and his companion were the only two people on the ride. So they couldn't get solace or company from other people's screams. Nor would they have probably been missed had they fallen out – until the bodies were found. A rollercoaster strategy of this kind can be just as bad, as you are not prepared for the sudden onrush of difficulty as implementation proceeds.

The difficulty-over-time curve can be plotted either for the total difficulty of the implementation activity or project, or for just one constraining force. The difficulty-over-time curve is most helpful when creating scenario storylines for implementation.

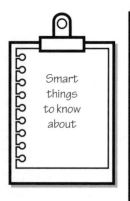

Smart
things
to know
about

THE DIFFICULTY-OVER-TIME CURVE

- It is dynamic, and helps to stretch our thinking about the future.
- It is easy to visualize mentally.
- It is easy to track divergence from expectations – so you do something differently.
- It has the following links to other techniques:
  - to force-field analysis – where it provides a visual way of thinking about the various forces through time;
  - to AID analysis – where it helps to think about to where a strategic project might shift; and
  - in conjunction with stakeholders – to examine how the difficulty of dealing with them is likely to change over time.

## Stakeholder analysis

Stakeholder analysis is another major tool for analysing implementation (Piercey, 1989; Grundy, 1993).

*Smart quotes*

Q: What is a stakeholder?

A: A stakeholder is an individual or group that has:

- a decision-making role;
- an advisory role;
- an implementing role; or
- a role as a user or victim.

Smart
answers to
tough
questions

Stakeholder analysis is performed as follows.

- First, identify who you believe the key stakeholders are at any phase of implementation.

- Second, evaluate whether these stakeholders have high, medium or low influence on the issue in question. (You need to abstract this from their influence generally in the organization.)

- Third, evaluate whether at the current time they are for the project, against it, or idling in neutral (see Fig. 7.6).

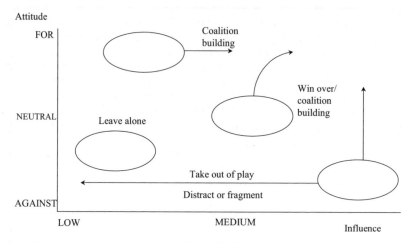

This tool is based on earlier versions by Piercy (1989)

**Fig. 7.6** Stakeholder analysis.

In order to see approximately where a stakeholder is positioned, you will need to see the world from that particular stakeholder's perspective. From experience over the years, we have found that the best way to convey this is to ask managers to have, in effect, an 'out-of-body' experience – but not quite literally, of course!

From experience, managers who literally do take the perspective that 'I am the stakeholder' are typically at least 50% more accurate in their analysis. This involves not merely trying to sense the surface attitudes of stakeholders to a particular issue, but also the deeper-seated emotions, focus, anxieties and even prejudices about the growth strategy. Figure 7.7 represents those levels which all need to be thought through.

Later on we illustrate how a specific stakeholder's agenda can be mapped using stakeholder agenda analysis, which is another application of force-field analysis.

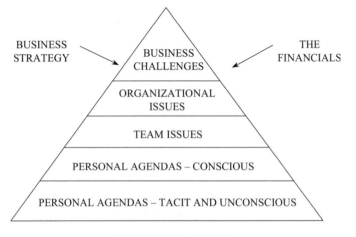

Fig. 7.7   Levels of agendas.

The above-mentioned three steps give a good 'first cut' of the pattern of stakeholders. The cluster of stakeholders depicted on a stakeholder grid (see Fig. 7.8) should then be assessed to see what the overall picture looks like, particularly:

- is the strategy an easy bet?;

- is it highlighting a long slog?; or

- does this seem like Mission Impossible?

For instance, if most of the stakeholders are clustered towards the bottom part of the stakeholder grid, then you clearly have a Mission Impossible on your hands (unless the stakeholders can be repositioned).

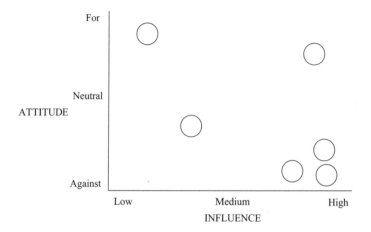

**Fig. 7.8** Stakeholder grid.

Another difficult configuration is where there is an equal number of supporting stakeholders (with lower influence) – i.e. in the north-west of the picture – to those against (but having higher influence) – in the south-east. Once again, this means that implementation is likely to experience major difficulties.

Finally, where you have a large number of stakeholders floating in neutral in the middle of the picture, this very neutrality can present major problems, due to organizational inertia.

It is a particularly useful idea to position yourself on the stakeholder grid, especially if you are the project manager. This helps you to re-examine your own position – and your underlying agendas – which may be mixed.

Following your tentative, first-cut analysis, you should then move on to the next phase, as follows.

- First, can new stakeholders be brought into play to shift the balance of influence or can existing players be withdrawn in some way (or be subtly distracted)?

- Second, is it possible to boost the influence of stakeholders who are currently in favour of the project?

- Third, is it possible to reduce the influence of any antagonistic stakeholders?

- Fourth, can coalitions of stakeholders in favour be achieved so as to strengthen their combined influence?

- Fifth, can coalitions of stakeholders antagonistic to the project be prevented?

- Sixth, can the project change itself, in appearance or in substance, be reformulated to diffuse hostility to it?

- Seventh, are there possibilities of 'bringing on board' any negative stakeholders, by allowing them a role or by incorporating one or more of their prized ideas?

- Eighth, is the pattern of influence of stakeholders sufficiently hostile for the project to warrant its redefinition?

*Case illustration – stakeholder analysis at a major bank*

A major financial institution was introducing some new processes that were fundamental to its operations. It decided to use the stakeholder analysis technique to identify who the key stakeholders on the project were and where they were likely to be positioned.

The half-day workshop began by identifying the key stakeholders. No less than 31 stakeholders were identified. At the end of the exercise the question was put: 'Who is the one big stakeholder that we have forgotten?' The answer was that there were actually two big stakeholders omitted – the customer and the media.

The moral: unless stakeholder analysis is used in strategic thinking, your implementation could easily fall over, as key players may be overlooked. Obviously, key stakeholders are likely to shift over time – and early support for the project may therefore evaporate. A number of things need to be anticipated, therefore.

- Senior managers' support is likely to be very sensitive to the perceived ongoing success of the strategic project as it evolves. Any signs of failure are likely to be accompanied by suddenly diminishing support.

- New stakeholders may enter the scheme, and others might disappear.

- Certain stakeholders may increase in influence, or even decrease in influence.

- Where the growth project changes significantly in its scope or focus, stakeholders will then change their positions.

- Stakeholders' own agendas might change due to external factors outside this particular project. For example, other projects might distract them or result in a reprioritization of agendas and of this project in particular.

STAKEHOLDER ANALYSIS

STAKEHOLDER ANALYSIS

Stakeholder analysis is useful:

- at the very start of a process of developing a growth strategy – even as early as the ideas stage;
- at the strategic options stage;
- when performing detailed planning;
- during mobilization of implementation;
- mid-way or at the latter stages of implementation; and
- after implementation – to draw out the key lessons.

Stakeholder analysis is also particularly useful for focusing on communication strategy. Here it will help you to identify which stakeholders to communicate with, when, how and with what message.

SMART THINGS TO DO

STAKEHOLDER ANALYSIS

- It deals effectively with the political issues associated with strategy.
- It encourages mental agility and the ability to take a variety of perspectives on an issue simultaneously (through the 'out-of-body' experience).
- It diffuses organizational politics and makes particularly sensitive issues discussible, sometimes called (by some colleagues at Cranfield) the 'Zone of Uncomfortable Debate' – or the 'ZUDE'.

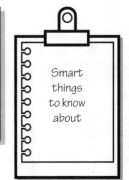

Smart things to know about

## Stakeholder agenda analysis

Stakeholder agenda analysis now helps you to go down a level deeper – to the agenda of a specific individual. Again we use the vector analysis format to explore this, distinguishing now between positive agendas (or 'turn-ons') versus negative agendas (the 'turn-offs') – see Fig. 7.9.

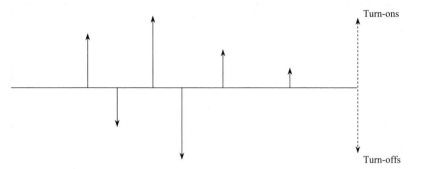

**Fig. 7.9** Stakeholder agenda analysis.

Stakeholder agenda analysis has a very high potential for frequent, everyday use. Besides being applied at a macro-level on the bigger strategic issues, it can be used on projects, for meetings generally and even for drafting a simple letter or e-mail or making a telephone call.

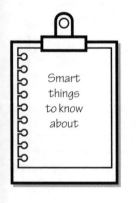

Smart
things
to know
about

STAKEHOLDER AGENDA ANALYSIS

- It can be used to help identify your own position on something and why you are in a dilemma.
- It helps you to make a business case or to make a strategic presentation.
- It can help you to get a new role – either inside or outside the organization.
- It can suggest what the deeper agendas of the organization are, so that you can target your activities in strategic thinking to the 'hotter spots' – thereby avoiding unnecessary frustration.

INTEGRATING GROWTH STRATEGIES

1 Growth issues need diagnosis and scoping before implementation – perhaps using the from-to (FT) techniques, or with advanced fishbone analysis (piranha analysis).
2 To make the link with implementation, how-how analysis and Gantt charts can help crystallize your growth project plan.
3 Force-field analysis gives a snapshot of likely implementation difficulty over a particular time period.
4 But it is ineffective unless you identify all the potential stoppers.
5 The difficulty-over-time curve helps you to think about difficulty in a more dynamic way.
6 Stakeholder analysis helps you to understand the level of current support, to position your growth project through influencing stakeholders and also to monitor shifts in their attitude and influences.
7 Stakeholder agenda analysis allows you to have the full 'out-of-body' experience of key stakeholders.

Smart
things
to know
about

# 8

# Valuing Growth Strategies

## *Introduction*

Why are growth strategies sometimes hard to evaluate? This chapter takes us through some of the most crucial issues, including:

- the three curses of value – dealing with interdependencies, intangibles and uncertainty;

- managing and measuring intangibles;

- value- and cost-driver analysis; and

- making an effective business case for growth.

### The three curses of value – interdependencies, intangibles and uncertainty

In a truly perfect world it would be possible to put an economic value on a growth strategy in terms that can be quantified in future cashflow. But in practical terms, quantitative analysis is frequently bogged down by difficulties. This is due to the three curses of value:

- interdependencies;

- intangibles; and

- uncertainty.

Interdependencies are problematic because of the difficulty of predicting how other interdependent parts of the organization and its outside environment will behave. Interdependencies fall into two categories – ones over which you have high influence and ones over which you have a lower influence. But even where you may think you have limited influence or control, you can often create it through the cunning plan.

The best way of dealing with interdependencies is to map – by way of a bubble diagram – the key systems on which the growth strategy may impact, and their most crucial interaction. The picture of the business value system for the football industry in Chapter 5 gives an excellent example of how to visualize interdependencies.

Where there are very many and complex interdependencies, this obviously makes the business more sensitive to disruption – and thus increases uncertainty and risk. For instance, in the mid-late 1990s Manchester United tried to push its merchandising growth strategy particularly hard. It diversified into products such as Manchester United whisky and Manchester United crisps – which one might have some difficulty in associating with what you might hope would be a healthy sport.

Some of these interdependencies can actually be monitored in terms of their impact on both value and cost drivers. For example, my own strategy consultancy work comes from a variety of sources, some from core customers, spin-offs from running strategy courses, through publications and via business school contracts or word of mouth. Over time, each of these sources of work can be identified – and both valued and costed – to see whether it looks economically viable, either directly or indirectly.

By mapping and interpreting these interdependencies in a creative, pictorial way, you should be able to get a better picture of how the value on a growth strategy is generated.

'And there was a business over there that had been completely neglected at head office. There was a flipchart in every office, which to me was a symptom of this very introverted style – the moment anybody had a meeting, someone was on a flipchart. The whole thing was driven by the processes rather than by the objectives. If there were objectives, they were tacked onto the process.

'People worked hard and interacted and interfaced, and essentially went around in circles. There was no questioning of "Why are we here?" or "What is the meaning of the universe?"

'I described it once as "This head office was once a great black hole which sucked energy out of the units. Things vanished into it never to be seen again". Whereas my idea of a head office is that it should be a tiny, tiny star in the sky, twinkling light down, completely out of the way.'

Lord Thurso, MD of Champneys

*Smart quotes*

## Managing and measuring intangibles

Intangibles are those areas of value which are not so concerned with inter-dependencies or uncertainty but with it being inherently difficult to put a value on. For many years, the financial assessment of intangibles was very primitive, until it was found (Grundy, 1992) that intangibles typically are a family of hard-to-value things. They have quite different characteristics, and therefore should be managed and measured differently.

Table 8.1 gives many clues as to how a value might be put on intangibles. By thinking about intangibles initially in a qualitative way, and only later in a quantitative way, a more realistic assessment is usually forthcoming.

We get more guidance on intangibles when we turn to the next main section on value and cost drivers, but here our next theme is that of uncertainty. We investigated the role of uncertainty analysis in some depth in Chapter 2 – using the uncertainty grids and scenario development.

It is imperative to draw up (as a minimum) an importance–uncertainty grid for the key assumptions which it is felt might have an impact on the value of the growth. Once this has been done, any financial sensitivity analysis should be done, principally for those assumptions which are both most important *and* most uncertain. Further, the extent of the sensitivity analysis should be done according to the perceived vulnerability of the growth strategy. (Arbitrary percentage sensitives of 5%, 10% and 15% should be avoided.)

We already saw the impact of the uncertainty grid in the BMW case. BMW presumably believed that acquiring Rover would generate an incremental vale of perhaps £1bn or more. This, sadly, turned into shareholder value destruction of around £3bn.

**Table 8.1**  Types of intangibles and possible measures.

| Types of intangibles | Related to other appraisal problems | Possible focus for measurement |
|---|---|---|
| Product image | Customer value | Customer views of product |
| Reduced customer product and service | Customer value | Customer views of costs and risks |
| Customer loyalty | Customer value | Estimated revenue and likelihood of switching |
| Protection of business | Protective investment | Monitoring incidence of existing loss of business |
| Spin-off opportunity | Contingent value and interdependency | Specify conditions under which opportunity arises is harvested |
| Flexibility | External and internal interdependency | Specify conditions under which flexibility will add value |
| Cost savings elsewhere | Internal interdependency | 'Before' and 'after' measurement of cost drivers and of impact |
| Alignment of external and internal factors | External and internal interdependency | Specification of conditions under which alignment may occur and probable value |

A summary of key questions for evaluating intangibles is therefore as follows.

1 Does much of the value of the opportunity depend on less tangible forces?

2 If so, are these factors measurable at some future point in time in financial terms, or not?

3 Where these are difficult to quantify financially, even at some future date, are there other ways of quantifying or assessing whether benefits have been realized (e.g. in market-based or operational measures)?

4 If so, is there an 'appropriate worth' that managers would be prepared to pay for these (or alternatively, if they had them, what would they pay to retain them – i.e. what is their 'deprival value')?

5 Are these benefits difficult to evaluate because they are, in effect, consumed externally (e.g. by customers)? If so, are these capable of being harvested by extra prices, or by avoiding price reduction, or by avoiding a loss of volume which might otherwise occur?

6 Have all areas of less tangible costs been included in the appraisal (e.g. does going ahead with the project result in difficult-to-quantify distraction costs as the business becomes increasingly complex)?

7 Where no formal value is put on intangibles, how is it proposed to reflect this value in the decision process, especially where there are tight financial constraints in place?

8 How will the less tangible factors subsequently be measured (e.g. by measuring service levels, customer perceptions, employee perceptions, etc.)?

9 Under what specific circumstances will assumed 'synergies' be harvested and how can these be measured?

10 Has future and 'contingent' opportunity that may spin off from the project been included and, if so, how?

11 Also, might the project foreclose other opportunities of significant value and what, therefore, is the contingent value lost by the opportunity?

Many strategies for growth are justified on the back of intangibles (at least in part), so it is particularly necessary to ensure that they are thought through and probed as rigorously as possible.

*Integrative case – Alton Towers and the zebra feature*

The following case records a conversation at a conference (for accountants) on the topic of linking strategy and value. At the coffee break, one accountant rushed up to one of the speakers to ask a burning question about a proposed area for breakthrough, He said:

*'I'm the accountant for a stately home which is open to the public. The owner has a small zoo and has asked me to financially evaluate a new project – to add a zebra feature. The question is this: how do I set about doing the incremental cashflows?'*

The accountant had fallen into the classic trap of trying to do the numbers before thinking through the strategy and impact on both competitive position and the operational effects. The speaker responded:

*'First, it seems to me that you have not really defined the problem or opportunity. Why do you need a zebra feature? Is it because visitors have said things like "What a nice little zoo – the crocodiles, the llamas, the monkeys, but where on earth was the zebra?" – and go away patently disappointed?*

*'Or was this just thought of as a nice-to-do? Or was it part of a bigger grand plan (effectively a strategic project set) to reposition the estate as a kind of mini-Longleat (a safari park bristling with zebras and lions) or even a Chessington World of Adventures (with lots of animals hanging around, looking rather redundant, while the visitors go on some scary theme park rides and water chutes)?*

*'I think it is an example of where you need to think through the project in terms of its degrees of competitive and financial advantage.*

*'Basically, a single lonely zebra is not likely to do an awful lot for the estate. It will add costs whilst not necessarily adding to customer satisfaction. In turn, this means you will not be able to justify any assumed benefits by way of increased volume of visitors or any price increase.*

*'But if you were to increase the project's competitive advantage quite considerably by say:*

- *adding a whole new jungle feature;*

- *and a mini-train to take visitors around it (without fear of being gobbled or pawed by the lions);*

- *advertising this as a unique 'stay alive – but in the jungle' feature*

*then there is just a hope of either getting more visitors throughput or increasing prices, or both.'*

The zebra example highlights how managers often fail to grapple with uncertainties, intangibles and interdependencies because they don't apply sufficient strategic thinking about the particular project. This strategic thinking can and must be sharpened up by detailed financial analysis.

But what about Alton Towers, which is arguably the UK's most developed theme park and the only one credibly claiming 'world-class' status (a kind of miniature Disney park)? Supposing you are the accountant of Alton Towers and are asked to present a business case for a new feature – say, the Nemesis ride. This ride has to be seen to be believed – it is truly a breakthrough feature which has repositioned Alton Towers in the popular imagination. Some brief facts on Nemesis are as follows.

- It was to be incorporated within an existing theme area of the park – the 'Forbidden Valley' – where Alton Towers already has a number of very exciting, if nasty, rides.

- Other main theme areas were: the Gloomy Wood; Katanga Canyon; Festival Park; the gardens; the Towers; Tower Street; the Land of Make Believe; and Fantasy World.

- The Nemesis ride lasts for around a minute, during which time the victims will loop the loop several times, rush through a canyon at great speed (almost hitting a smoking bus) and then come to an abrupt halt.

My daughter would like to add a little to this case study:

*'I wasn't sure that I would actually go on it – the hour-and-a-half queue gives you lots of opportunity to have doubts … You don't really see anything – the world just spins around as you feel you are coming out of your seat … especially if you are small, like me. It feels like seconds but it gives a lasting memory … you feel really ill – sick with excitement.'*

The unique selling proposition of the Nemesis project is thus fear, and fear, in this case, is a growth driver. This is maximized by having riders dangling their legs from their seat into thin air. There will be no physical security, as is found, say, in sitting in a runaway train or on a normal ride.

The benefits of the Nemesis project (which is going to be really quite expensive, considering the huge engineering works) are:

- it will measurably increase the flood of visitors to the park, eager to try the Nemesis experience; and

- it will, at the same time, add to capacity by distracting visitors from other, tamer, experiences that are quite busy.

The actual results of Nemesis exceeded Alton Towers' expectations. In the first spring of Nemesis, other areas of the park became eerily quiet as visitors queued for between one and three hours to go on the ride. Really lucky visitors actually went on it three times in one day. In fact the ride was almost too successful in its first year, virtually unbalancing the flow of visitors through the park.

This attraction resulted in a measurable incremental flow of visitors to the park, and thus in significant growth. It would certainly have done much to prevent any erosion of trade that might otherwise have occurred (the declining-base case). It was also of major intangible benefit, helping build the Alton Towers name outside its traditional core market (most UK managers have by now heard of the ride and some have even thought about going on it as the ultimate experience in turbulence).

But there are other issues too. I discreetly asked at the end of a particular season what new and bigger ride was in store for the next year. The answer was that only one of the older rides was being replaced. I felt let down. Over the last three years there has been a new ride to resuscitate interest and demand. With any successful strategy for growth, you always need to ask what the encore will be. Since then, Alton Towers has implemented a new growth driver on this scale, 'Oblivion', which produces a near-death experience.

The Alton Towers case highlights once again the need to think through:

- the way in which value is created as part of a system of business activities;

- the internal and external interdependencies (both now and in the future);

- the importance of building, and then harvesting, intangibles;

- the need to juggle with competitive, operational and financial advantages through time in strategic development; and

- the importance of separating out (like the zebra feature case) different 'states of the world' for financial evaluation. States of the world that are too similar in terms of the levels of advantage offered will be very hard indeed to evaluate financially.

## Value- and cost-driver analysis

Value- and cost-driver analysis helps us to get a better steer on the 'attractiveness' of a particular strategic breakthrough. A value driver is defined as 'anything outside or inside the business which either directly or indirectly will generate cash inflows – either now or in the future'. A cost driver is defined as 'anything outside or inside the business which either directly or indirectly will generate cash outflows – either now or in the future'.

Examples of value drivers include:

- customer loyalty;

- a lack of competitive pressure;

- a unique product; and

Smart
things
to know
about

VALUE DRIVERS

They can always be turned into cash – one day and in one way or another.

- a value-creating technology.

Examples of cost drivers include:

- complexity of operations;

- poor quality; and

- bureaucratic processes and structures.

Figures 8.1 and 8.2, which depict a value- and cost-driver analysis for supermarket trolleys, is an excellent example of this. Here we see the value drivers being split down into 'value to the customer' and 'company value' – to give the macro-level value drivers. The macro cost drivers have a different split, these being analysed over the new wonder-trolleys' life-cycle of costs. Other cuts to the cost analysis are:

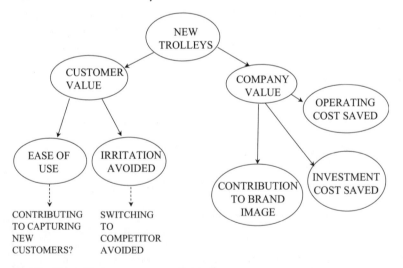

**Fig. 8.1**  Value drivers – new supermarket trolleys.

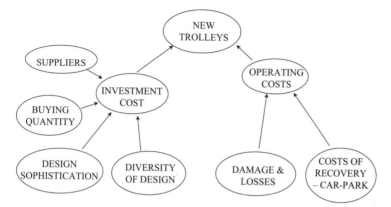

Fig. 8.2   Cost drivers – new supermarket trolleys.

- cost by activity;

- cost by process; and

- cost through the transaction cycle.

Most managers using value- and cost-driver analysis for the first time tend to copy relatively slavishly whatever example is given to them. Whilst this usually comes off, it is important to realize that the structure of value and cost drivers will vary according to the specific situation.

To illustrate this, let us look at a second example. In Figs 8.3 and 8.4 we see the value and cost drivers of our (small) consultancy, potentially investing in a website in 1999. We were sceptical as to its potential value (at that time), not only in terms of 'Will we get more business?' but also 'Will it be the quality we are targeting?' Also, being very busy already, the obvious point was how we would accommodate much more work.

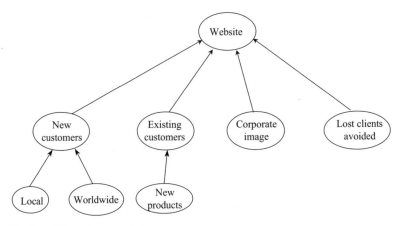

**Fig. 8.3** Value drivers – website.

This value- and cost-driver analysis was done in around six minutes in a café in Edinburgh, overlooking the castle. Tea and croissants were consumed simultaneously, highlighting the fact that these analyses can be done very, very quickly. The figures were illuminating. The key insights (which were not there before) were as follows.

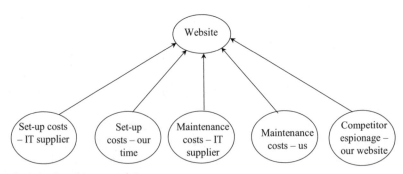

**Fig. 8.4** Cost drivers – website.

- More value was likely to be added (at least in the medium term) from selling more to existing clients (by getting them to look at our website) rather than by new hits.

- New hits might come from companies that were geographically distant, costing more in travel time and inconvenience.

- The costs of maintaining the website could exceed set-up costs, as would the cost of our time to input into the design.

- There were considerable downside costs, through competitors seeking to copy our products.

- The protective value was intriguing – if one did not have a website, how would one track lost business to competitors with websites?

On the basis of the final bullet point above, we decided to continue to monitor this possibility closely but not to go ahead yet.

Value- and cost-driver analysis is essential for anyone doing a business case, especially before doing the financial numbers. (Imagine how wrong our numbers would have been had we not done this analysis!) Its key benefits are:

- it provides a key bridge between strategy and finance;

- it helps to stretch thinking laterally about less obvious areas of value and cost; and

- it is highly flexible.

## Making an effective business case for growth

When someone says the words 'business case' most managers think of a weighty, detailed document (or doorstop?) with lots of hard facts and figures. In larger companies, managers typically see this as a necessary evil – required to get a release of investment funds – within an adversarial environment. Some want to run for the hills (or even away to Alton Towers).

But the real point of a business case is to gain more clarity about the objectives of the project, its implications for the business, and particularly to expose and test the key assumptions which drive value. This can be achieved in a very succinct way by, for instance, restricting the business case to a maximum of eight pages, as noted below (often, fewer pages will suffice). All of our work might be to no avail if we were unable to produce an effective business case at the end of it.

Whilst we have introduced you to a number of useful analysis techniques, it is not necessarily the case that we should *always* use them in presentation. Instead of being a victim of content and detail, you should focus backwards from the main point of the presentation – based on a top management problem. In the course of this work (either orally or written) it may be useful to provide both structure and flow to your argument or display a number of the techniques. For example, the techniques in Table 8.2 could be used.

Remember, the golden rule must always be: look at the world through the eyes of the other stakeholders (and have the out-of-body experience again).

A useful format for a business case is as follows.

- Executive summary (1 page).

- Project definition, objectives and scope (1 page).

**Table 8.2** Techniques for making an effective business case for growth.

| The need | The techniques |
| --- | --- |
| To highlight the growth's overall attractiveness | The strategic option grid, supported (as necessary) by bottom-up techniques |
| To analyse financial attractiveness | Value and cost drivers |
| To communicate the implications | FT analysis |
| To prioritize individual areas of action | The AID grid |
| To test for possible uncertainty | The uncertainty grid |
| To help surface agendas and to influence | Stakeholder analysis |

- How the project adds value (new opportunity, tangible synergy, defensive or protective value) (1 page).

- Key external and internal assumptions (with an evaluation of importance and uncertainty) (3 pages).

- Implementation issues (1 page).

- Summary financials (1 page).

This brings the total length to eight pages, plus detailed appendices containing technical details, detailed financial and non-financial measures and milestones, detailed financial sensitivities, detailed resource requirements – possibly another seven pages. This brings a typical case to just 15 pages.

Business cases will therefore only add value if they:

- are clear, succinct and written in a jargon-free style;

- expose the most important and uncertain assumptions, and address these both in the sensitivity analysis and via contingency planning;

- do not fall into the trap of seeing the financial numbers as absolute measures of value, but use them creatively. For instance, in dealing with fewer tangibles it may be fruitful to put an illustrative value on 'what these might be worth', so that a more balanced, overall appraisal of the project can be achieved.

Managers may well find it difficult to justify including a quantified value within a business case for a contingent project unless at least the balance of probabilities were in its favour (one might speculate that this level of probability may be, say, over 50%, or even 75%, depending upon how managers apply control measures).

There may also be a further cut-off point, at which level of perceived probability a contingent event is deemed to be worthwhile, including within any qualitative assessment of value (that is, as an upside to the business case). One way of coping with this is to distinguish between:

- demand that is *conceivable* – it is relatively indeterminate, as buyers may not have defined intent to buy something at all, nor what their specific needs might be;

- demand that is *contingent* – buyers are becoming clearer that they will have a need that will require satisfaction but they are unclear how best to meet that need; and

- demand that has *crystallized* – buyers have made a clear commitment to a course of action, either through explicit decision or through establishing a predictable pattern of buying.

Estimating the value of opportunities that are based on conceivable demand appears to be best addressed by broad-brush thinking. This might involve exploring the overall shape and size of market demand and potential advantage of the product, given some view of competitor intent and insight into likely customer requirement. Where demand is contingent, a firmer estimate of demand might be assessable through more in-depth market analysis as the shape of demand firms up.

Where, however, demand is contingent or conceivable, there may be severe boundaries to the use of financial appraisal tools. This is, perhaps, the territory of the 'unknowable'. In this case, managers may find the use of techniques such as net present value (NPV) to have a 'fraudulent feel' – unless of course they are aware that such measures are illustrative only. NPV would still be useful as a tool here, as it would be possible to work backwards to explore the kind of market conditions in which a positive NPV would appear viable (rather than using market and operational assumptions to generate the NPV).

To summarize, key questions to help value projects with contingent value are as follows.

- In what circumstances can value actually occur, and how remote are these circumstances?

- What steps can be taken to help crystallize value, or to avoid events which will prevent value from crystallizing?

- What makes the company think it will be well placed competitively to exploit the opportunity when it actually crystallizes?

- Is it appropriate to include an estimated value in the business case, an illustrative value (based on a 'what if?') or simply a qualitative statement about value, as the use of formal NPV may be perceived as misleading?

*Joint ventures*

Joint ventures and other collaborative arrangements are often fruitful avenues for growth. Joint venture projects typically (but not always) involve
smaller investment outlays, but greater risks in terms of the sustainability
of income. The literature on joint ventures (for instance, Lorange & Roos,
1992) suggest that joint ventures:

- are highly competitive arrangements, where parties seek to maximize
  the leverage which they get out of the joint venture. This is done while
  revealing their own core competencies only to a minimum;

- are characterized in the early stages with 'things going well', followed by
  a period of increasing instability, which precedes break down;

- rarely survive beyond around six years without one partner becoming
  dominant.

Joint ventures thus present special problems of appraisal. Frequently, they
appear to generate very attractive NPVs and high internal rates of return
(IRRs). But this is perhaps due to projected cashflows being based on 'everything going right', instead of the high-risk scenarios painted earlier.

Joint ventures offer a rare possibility for using decision-tree analysis to
explore different turns of events (with probability and payoff assessments).
Table 8.3 shows an example.

The expected NPV of £8.5mn compares unfavourably against a simplistic
NPV of the first five years of £5m plus the rest of life of £8m, or £13m.

**Table 8.3**   Decision-tree analysis – joint venture.

| | |
|---|---|
| First five years NPV | £5mn |
| After five years – 50% probability of becoming dominant partner: expected value (rest of life) 50% × £8mn | £4mn |
| 20% probability of being bought out: expected value (sale of shares) 20% × £5mn | £1mn |
| 30% probability of the joint venture collapsing in acrimony 30% × £5mn | (£1.5mn) |
| Total expected NPV | £8.5mn |

## Exit strategies

Finally, exit from a business is frequently a strategic decision just as much as entry. Although accountants and managers appreciate the need to evaluate the incremental cashflows of new businesses, it is rare to see them challenge existing businesses or projects.

Sometimes the 'exit option' occurs when managers have been considering a new investment project within an existing business. When evaluating the financial projections, it becomes increasingly evident that the project is being pushed uphill, struggling to achieve justification. This can sometimes be because the business itself is in steep strategic and financial decline.

Another trigger to business reappraisal may occur because corporate-level management are uncomfortable with the strategic plans of a business. Despite its marketplace being fundamentally unattractive (very competitive, mature and low-growth) and its competitive position being suspect, its financial plans still seem rosy. By appraising the business as a strategic project (using discounted cashflow), managers may be forced to:

- stretch their strategic thinking further out into the future than, say, just three years;

- understand the challenge of where any positive NPV is coming from; and/or

- surface and challenge the key competitive and other external assumptions on which NPV is based.

In some instances, reappraisal may reveal that the business is not currently contributing to shareholder value and that it may be worth more to another parent. In other instances, regeneration options are flushed out and prevent the business from being starved of fresh investment.

We have argued the need to understand the key value drivers, and to expose and challenge the key assumptions before undertaking the sensitivity analysis. 'Better practice' means doing very rigorous testing of those key variables which are likely to be most uncertain and most important. If needs be, for instance, one might reduce prices by, say, 5% to reflect competitive rivalry and new entrants. (Coincidentally, this is the exact reduction in nominal prices in the early to mid-1990s in the UK supermarket industry – something perhaps unthinkable before the event.)

It is only by working this way around that true sensitivity analysis is performed, otherwise all you end up with is 'insensitivity analysis' – playing with the assumption set to get the right answer: a positive NPV (which in this case means no more than 'numbers prevent vision').

Finally, an important issue is how to deal with the terminal value. This is the value which is put on the cash plans at the end of the time horizon of the projections. With slow payback decisions the terminal value can amount to between 40% and 50% of NPV. Yet terminal value may be subject to minimal strategic and financial scrutiny. Invariably, terminal values can be proved more effectively using a quick competitive and financial scenario, which, although broad-brush, checks that the assumptions prima facie make sense.

Key questions for compiling an effective business case are therefore as follows.

1 Does the business case specify clearly the scope and objectives of the strategic development project, its relationship to other areas of investment (capital or revenue) and to operational change?

2 Does it specify what the strategic routes to value creation are – e.g. competitive enhancement or protection versus synergistic value, or creating future spin-off opportunities?

3 Are key strategic operational and financial assumptions clearly identified?

4 Are key uncertainties and interdependencies identified?

5 Does the 'sensitivity analysis' focus on key risks and also on exploring worst downsides (and also any upsides that may strain capacity and push up unit-cost levels)?

6 Has break-even analysis been conducted to test the robustness of NPV, and does this take each of the high-impact external and internal assumptions in turn?

7 Have areas of 'softer' value – including intangibles, the protective value from slowing a declining-base case or the value of contingent and future opportunity – been identified and, if necessary, isolated in the business case?

8  If the project is targeted at achieving a shorter payback, would this produce some useful reshaping of the 'project definition'?

9  Besides IRR (i.e. that discount rate at which there is a zero NPV), has NPV also been assessed in order to prioritize projects and has the NPV been compared across projects along with variations in payback? (All other things being equal, a project with faster payback may be preferable to another project with similar NPV.)

10  What is the basis for any 'terminal' or residual vale which has been included?

11  How does this project affect the total financial balance of the portfolio of projects (or businesses), given its cashflow profile?

12  What is the likely impact on bottom-line earnings? Is this such that the proposal needs to be 'sold' back to the shareholders to highlight longer-term benefits and to shift these perceived constraints?

13  What operational and organizational requirements are required to implement the project satisfactorily?

14  Have the 'critical success factors' of successful implementation been fully thought through?

VALUING GROWTH STRATEGIES

1  Interdependencies, intangibles and uncertainty are the biggest causes of problems in valuing growth.
2  Interdependencies need to be mapped out, to understand how they operate as a system.
3  Intangibles need to be broken down into categories, and dealt with in a case-by-case way.
4  Uncertainties should be addressed through the uncertainty grids (see Chapter 2).
5  Value and cost drivers help to trade off value versus cost.
6  They also help us to understand intangibles much better.
7  Business cases and business plans need to be succinct, have a clear logic and expose (rather then bury) those most uncertain assumptions – to open up the debate.

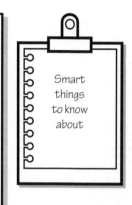

Smart things to know about

# 9

# Growth Checklists

## *Introduction*

The following growth checklists will assist you in thinking through growth strategies. This chapter covers:

- organic growth;

- acquisitions;

- franchises;

- international;

- the Internet; and

- organizational capability:

- restructuring projects; and
- information systems projects.

THE GROWTH CHECKLISTS

They can be used:

- as pre-work before growth workshops;
- to help structure the key questions in growth workshops;
- to help identify the 'One Big Thing' that we have forgotten;
- to target data collection;
- during the ongoing management of growth; and
- to post-appraise and learn from past growth strategies.

## *Organic growth*

This section takes you through:

- product growth projects;

- market growth projects;

- selling more to existing customers;

- new value-creating activities;

- new distribution channels; and

- new technologies.

*Product growth projects*

The following questions deal with product development as a vehicle for organic growth.

1 How fast is the market for this type of product growing?

2 How much competitive pressure exists in its market?

3 How well does the product meet its target customer needs – what are the turn-ons and turn-offs from a customer point of view?

4 Which other products is it competing with and what are the relative advantages/disadvantages between each?

5 How (if at all) does the product need servicing, and what are the relative competitive advantages here?

6 How complex is the product, and will this level of complexity mean that it is (a) harder to launch or (b) less flexible to change subsequently?

7 Are there any wonderfully innovative features of the product (which add real value)?

8 If these exist, how easily can these be imitated?

9 How consistent is the organization's capability and mindset with this product, and what implementation issues might this raise?

10 What skills training is required to support this product effectively?

11 Are the product's long-run unit costs likely to be sustainable in the longer-term?

12 What other changes are needed in the organization (for example, to key business processes or to organizational structure)?

13 Will the sales force and distribution channels accommodate the new product effectively – without destruction, disruption or a dilution of sales of other products?

14 To what extent might the product cannibalize other existing products?

15 To what extent will the product's innovation be project managed well?

16 How can its introduction be positioned and accelerated in the organization?

## Market growth projects

New market-led growth projects may overlap to some extent with new products. Nevertheless, we include some new questions below to supplement those on new products.

1 Have you systematically prioritized which (of the potential new markets) it would be most attractive to address (for example, using AID analysis or the strategic option grid)?

2 How inherently attractive is this market (consider its growth drivers and the level of competitive pressure in it)?

3 How difficult is it to operate within that market (generally)?

4 Do we have the natural competencies to do well in this market?

5 Is this market culturally vastly different from our current core markets?

6 Is this a market especially prone to discounting, high costs of satisfying customers or distribution channels, or low margins generally?

7 Have we got a genuinely 'cunning' entry strategy (or just an average one)?

8 What channel strategy options exist and which of these is (a) most inherently attractive (in terms of its use and value added generally) and (b) one where we have greatest competitive advantage?

9 What are the most critical uncertainties about that market and how can we minimize our exposure to them?

10 Will entering this particular market foreclose options to enter other markets?

11 To what extent will market conditions vary internationally, and which of these markets should we really give highest priority?

## Selling more to existing customers

Selling more to our existing customers may well be a neglected growth strategy, but nevertheless one which might be both highly attractive and relatively easy.

1 Which parts of our existing customer base could we potentially sell more to?

2 What could we sell them, why and how?

3 What things have prevented us in the past from selling as much as our true potential to existing customers?

4 What latent, existing needs could we satisfy – and which are we not currently satisfying?

5 What latent, future needs could we satisfy – and how?

6 How might selling more to our existing customers strengthen our relationship with them and gain lock-in?

7 Are there other buyers within the customer's organization to whom we can sell (e.g. another management function, another division, etc.)?

8 What specific sales or other incentives would encourage greater penetration of our existing customer base?

9 Which of our key competitors is currently active within these customers and how can we erode their share?

10 How can we make it unbelievably easy to buy from us (and to buy more from us)?

11 How can these improvements be project managed?

## New value-creating activities

Adding value in new ways may offer exciting project opportunities but ones which managers may find it difficult to think through.

1   Are there new ways in which we can add value to the customer (value-creating activities)?

2   How much additional value is likely to be created for them – from their perspective?

3   How will we be able to capture or share this value creation, given our relative bargaining power and our longer-term strategy?

4   To what extent should new value-creating activities be in- or out-sourced, and why?

5   How readily might new ways of adding value be imitated by competitors?

6   To what extent will customers seek to do these value-creating activities themselves (assuming they are worthwhile having)?

7   What is our natural level of competence for adding value in these new ways?

8   Can we easily pilot these new value-creating opportunities?

9   How will we project manage developing these new value-creating activities?

## New distribution channels

Opening up new distribution channels avoids the difficulties of new product and/or market innovation – and may well be cheap. But in order to avoid diluting our strategy and shareholder value, we will need to be relatively selective.

1 How much margin are we likely to obtain from a new distribution channel?

2 How difficult is it likely to be to deal with?

3 What are the key alternatives to dealing with this particular channel (for example, by the Internet, sales force, an alliance, etc.)?

4 Will this particular channel lead to conflict with any other distribution channels and, if so, how will we manage it?

5 Are we likely to get a high level of returns or other quality problems through this channel?

6 Will the channel actually understand our product sufficiently well?

7 How much support will this channel put behind our product – relative to that of other products?

8 Does this distribution channel have something that fits our natural competencies and our culture?

9 How competitive is this particular channel relative to other pathways to market?

10 If we do not use this channel, what (if anything) is the biggest down-side?

11 How would we project manage new entry to this channel?

## New technologies

New technologies may be a turn-on to middle managers but a turn-off to top managers (whose main focus is to extract short- and medium-term values out of the business). We may therefore need some testing questions in order to screen innovative technology growth projects.

1 Does the technology actually fit with our present or emerging definition of 'What Business(es) We Are In'?

2 Do we really understand the technology?

3 What other things (other than technology) all have to line up to deliver real value? (Use wishbone analysis.)

4 Are we doing the project mainly because of its sheer technological edge, and because it is inherently exciting, or because it will generate real value, and value that we can actually harvest?

5 What key value and cost drivers are impacted on by the new technology?

6 What new skills do we need to fully exploit any new technology?

7 To what extent do we have to change our mindset in order to get the very best out of the new technology?

8 Where the technology relies heavily on the Internet, how easily is our business model copied or imitated?

9 How quickly will the new technology spread, and, where there are customer turn-offs in its use, how can these be mitigated or removed?

10 How rapidly might the technology be superseded by further technologies and how vulnerable does this therefore make our strategy?

11 What substitute technologies are available which are in many respects better right now?

12 How should we project manage the introduction of the new technology?

## Acquisitions

1 Have you fully understood your own strategic position *before* embarking on the acquisition route?

2 What other options (over and above acquisitions) have you also considered, and how did these appear on the strategic option grid?

3 What does doing a GE grid analysis of the target's business positioning suggest about the inherent value (V1) of the acquisition?

4 What makes you confident that the bargaining context and process lead you into overpaying (and thus having a negative V1)?

5 What particular clever integration plans do you have and how will you implement these effectively (again, avoiding negative V1)?

6 What might be the reaction of customers, competitors and suppliers, should you make the acquisition?

7 What approach do you have to making appropriate changes within the target's management team, and what are the potential impacts of this?

8 Have you understood the extent of investment required not just to grow the business but to prevent, or make up for, competitive decline?

9 What are the key assumptions which you are implicitly making to support 'the acquisition going beautifully well' – how do these appear in the importance–uncertainty grid?

10 Despite all of this analysis, what is the 'One Big Thing' that we have forgotten?

## Alliances and joint venture projects

Whilst acquisitions capture the headlines in the financial press, many organizations move their corporate strategy forward in a slightly more stealthy fashion through alliances (otherwise known as 'joint ventures'). A 'strategic alliance' can now be defined as: 'A longer-term strategic partnership between two or more organizations where there is investment in the venture by all of those partners, sharing both reward and risk.'

Alliances may be thought of as being less risky than acquisitions. It is true that often the exposure of an alliance partner may be less (due to sharing of risk and the fact that the commitment, although longer-term, is usually not quite so permanent). However, the riskiness of an alliance can be higher due to:

- the very looseness of the arrangements;

- the need for a good deal of co-operation and openness;

- the fact that alliance partners may often have different aspirations (and possibly ones in tension or conflict), or different levels of bargaining power;

- the strategies of partners may change over time (and alongside that, the personal agendas of key players in top management); and

- the alliance itself will evolve and change as will its competitive environment.

Having said the above, alliances can be extremely profitable – for example, witness Securicor's alliance with British Telecom to form the mobile telecommunications company Cellnet. Cellnet became so successful that Securicor's total shareholder value (as a group) was substantially increased, independently of performance in Securicor's traditional businesses.

Some key questions to reflect upon for any alliance (split up into the phases of formation and development) are as follows.

### Formation

1 What is the fundamental purpose of the alliance – what distinctive value does it add?

2 Why is it likely to be better than other possible alliances?

3 What are the different options for structuring and resourcing the alliance?

4 To what extent is the alliance well timed?

5 How are the various needs and competencies of the alliance partners genuinely complementary?

6 To what extent are these needs and competencies in tension or in potential conflict?

7 To what extent is the alliance genuinely (therefore) a 'positive sum game' (or an arrangement where all parties are significantly better off through participating in the alliance)?

8 What is the potential for the alliance leading on into a full acquisition, longer-term?

9 Culturally, are the alliance partners likely to get on with each other: well, satisfactorily or, perhaps, badly?

10 Have all partners got sufficient interest in and commitment to the alliance to make it genuinely effective?

11 Will our making an alliance with another partner(s) only give us a temporary advantage, in that it will trigger other alliances in the industry?

12 What are the potential risks and downsides of sustaining our core competencies by depending upon the alliance?

13 Can we learn about how our partners do things really well and apply them elsewhere in our business without our partners becoming antagonistic?

14 How long (realistically) do we think the alliance is likely to last?

15 Who (if anyone) is likely to become the more dominant partner in the alliance, and if this is not likely to be us, what is the potential value of us being in the alliance?

16 Do any arrangements for potential divorce adequately safeguard our interests?

17 How will the formation of the alliance be project managed?

## Development

1 What investment is the alliance likely to require over time, and are alliance partners both able and willing to commit this when the time arrives?

2 What senior management (and other scarce skills) is the alliance likely to need, and who will support this requirement?

3 How will alliance partners conduct any reviews of performance and steer the strategy forward?

4 In the event that the alliance takes off even more successfully than anticipated, how will it cope with this, particularly with regard to:
   • people;
   • structures; and
   • financial resources?

5 What processes are in place for the management of any change of partners (including new ones coming in, old ones leaving or changes in partner stakes)?

6 How will alliance development be project managed (for example, what will its key milestones be)?

## Franchises

Franchises offer a potentially interesting strategy for growth. They appear to offer most potential value where:

- there are significant benefits for standardization – in marketing, branding and service delivery;

- there are significant financial costs of entry, making it hard for a smaller business unit to survive on its own;

- there are significant financial benefits to the franchisor and franchisee – the franchisor typically has access to cheaper and more flexible finance than the franchisee, and the bargaining power of both stakeholders then determines how this value is shared;

- there are opportunities for 'sweat' value – through entrepreneurial drive, which would not be found in a larger organization (again, this value is shared by the various stakeholders); and/or

- retail and service sectors (including hotels and restaurants) often lend themselves to franchise-based growth.

Our checklists now cover the elements of franchises.

1   What is your brand strength, and what is its potential (this adds value to the franchise)?

2   How difficult and expensive will it be to enforce service standards, even given training?

3   What are the potential knock-on consequences of quality defects in service delivery (for example on customer loyalty and potential media coverage)?

4   Has this franchisee done something like it before?

5   Are they likely to have an appropriate mindset for your own?

6   How committed will they be to making it work?

7   What are the opportunity costs of going by the franchise route (for example, in limiting your future distribution)?

8   What are the value and cost drivers of the franchise arrangements, and how financially attractive do the arrangements look like being?

9   What scenario stories can you tell about the alliance:
    • going well in future; and
    • going not so well?

## International

The checklists on organic, acquisition and alliance-based growth are equally applicable to international growth. International development requires thinking through.

1  What kind of international business do we wish to have, and why?

2  What is our current position on a grid of inherent counting/market attractiveness versus competitive position (use an adapted 'GE' grid)?

3 Is our range of international activities likely to become widely complicated, and not act as an internal brake on growth?

4 Do we have customers who are genuinely international in scope, and how difficult will it be to serve them in practice?

5 What options exist other than international expansion – for example, agents, alliances, franchises or our own operations?

6 Which of the international growth-support processes or activities need to be managed on an international versus local level, and with what logic?

7 Do we need to develop a more international management mindset and skill set, and if so how?

8 Do we work comfortably in international project teams, where these are appropriate?

9 Do we have a good communications infrastructure for managing international growth?

10 Do we have the cross-cultural experience and sensitivity to manage any acquisitions or alliances?

11 Is taking ourselves internationally just too great a degree of diversification, given perhaps that it may also take us into new markets, possibly with new products?

12 Have we got the actual *commitment* to grow internationally?

13 What is likely to happen if we *do not* develop internationally?

## The Internet

The Internet potentially gives us further opportunities for growth over and above existing channels. The case study of Amazon.com in Chapter 1 is a graphic illustration of how Internet growth strategies are sometimes not what they seem at first sight. We also touched on this particular market in Chapter 2 when we covered external growth drivers. The Internet appears to have more impelling opportunities for growth (in the short and medium term) in the business-to-business market, rather then in end-customer business and retail.

Many of the questions that we have asked around organic growth also apply here – but in a tailored way, as follows.

1  What is the impelling basis of customer demand – in terms of variety, search possibilities, reliability of fulfilment, cost, speed of delivery, etc.?

2  Is this sufficient to create a question on competitive advantage vis-à-vis existing fulfilment, given the penetration of market segments which can be realistically addressed?

3  How does the Internet encourage customer loyalty and lock-in?

4  To what extent does the Internet increase the bargaining power of buyers, and the rivalry amongst the competitors, and turn them into a commodity (especially in a more mature market)?

5  Will customers make orders in sufficiently economic quantities for us to make money?

6  What things will really turn-on the customer to Internet ordering, and what will distinctively turn them off?

7 How much will it cost (realistically) to create and update a website?

8 What are the competitors up to in this area and how might they leapfrog us?

9 What are the entry barriers likely to be (if they are very low then this will lead to less quality growth)?

10 How can we increase these entry barriers over others?

11 When do we expect the operation to generate an economic project, and is this a realistic expectation?

12 Have we seen fit to manage this development as a breakthrough growth project?

## Organizational capability

The next two sections break down between using restructuring and information systems development.

### Restructuring projects

Restructuring projects are now undertaken on an almost routine basis by most larger organizations. Restructuring is often managed in relative isolation from other projects and is also positioned as geared towards delivering more shorter-term benefits. Restructuring can be handled much more effectively than this, especially if the following questions are addressed.

1   Is the rationale for the restructuring fully thought through and does this not merely reflect current needs but anticipate pending changes in the business?

2   Is there a history of frequent restructuring which has resulted in a permanent (and unnecessary) state of instability in the organization? If so, how can this be managed more strategically in the future?

3   Has the restructuring put managers into 'artificial' positions without genuine business benefits, which are patently transparent and which will aggravate organizational ambiguity?

4   Are new appointees genuinely capable of being effective in their roles, given their skills, their style and the degree of team-working within the organization?

5   Has the restructuring been communicated in such a way as to lay bare the business-led reasons for the restructuring?

6   What is the timing of announcement of the restructuring – has it been deliberately timed so as to prevent reflection and debate and thereby result in simmering resentment?

7   How does the restructuring complement other projects or initiatives in the business and how should it be managed alongside these?

## Information systems projects

Life in today's organizations is almost unrecognizable with the expansion of office technology and communications. Information systems are demanding at a business, technical, cultural and especially an interpersonal level. Therefore, consider the following questions.

1 Are all projects aimed at changing information systems part of an overall information strategy that is, in turn, linked to both business strategy and intended organizational change?

2 How have the costs/benefits of any systems project been evaluated in terms of both internal and external benefits and costs, including:
- customer value;
- access to markets;
- customer 'lock-in';
- improving responsiveness; and
- operational efficiency and capacity?

3 Are changes in information systems seen as (a) primarily a technical issue or (b) as also generating important and more difficult people-related and political issues? In the latter case, does the organization have the necessary tools (like stakeholder analysis) and processes to gain maximum ownership for change?

4 Who are the key stakeholders, both of the end outputs of information systems and in terms of agents within the change process itself?

5 Is there a risk of overrun against required timescales that might result in an expensive and disruptive 'crash programme' or a dilution of project benefits?

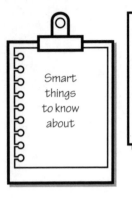

GROWTH CHECKLISTS

- You can't only keep things inside your brain – do use the checklists!
- Adopt them in your own growth processes.
- Each individual area of growth demands quite specific consideration (the checklists are quite different).
- Use these as tailored support when evaluating key options with the strategic option grid.

# 10
# Conclusion

## *Résumé of the key lessons of the book*

Growth is not something that falls out of the annual planning exercise, nor out of monthly management meetings. It needs to be thought about strategically and debated fully within the management team – and in a relatively structured way.

Whilst there are many successful *emergent* growth strategies, there are perhaps rather more that have failed (or become 'submergent'). We should therefore look to creating growth through deliberate process, rather than just by serendipity.

The key lessons of the book are perhaps best summarized in seven learning points as follows.

## Learning point 1 – growth is a dynamic process

Growth is a dynamic, ongoing process – and thus requires continuous reflection and review, rather than being deep-frozen in annual business plans. Growth is a never-ending journey with sometimes unpredictable twists and turns. Who would have imagined, for example, that Virgin, which started in the music business, would start up a transatlantic airline and go into banking and mobile phones? Nevertheless, at each juncture strategic choices were made, and ones which were costly or even impossible to reverse.

This uncertainty of direction actually argues for *more* emphasis on strategic thinking, rather then less. Annual plans should not be seen as the main occasion when thinking about growth is done. Rather, they should serve merely to set down snapshot cumulative thinking up to that point in time.

## Learning point 2 – growth requires imagination

Sustainable growth will only come in the long term by creative use of the imagination. For particular periods of time, markets do expand, and sometimes quite rapidly, almost without the active intervention of suppliers in that market. But in the longer term, few markets will be able to sustain more than modest rates of growth. Also, a good deal of growth is cyclical – most markets are immune to economic slowdown, which puts major and disproportionate pressure on less innovative companies.

In the cases of Dyson, Manchester United and the funerals business, we saw how innovations in the business model can transform the growth possibilities for a company – and thus financial returns.

## Learning point 3 – 'culturate' your growth mindset

Growth requires competing through your own mindset. By being able to let go of the current industry (and company) mindset, it becomes easier to think about how you might reach a superior growth path. Each industry (and the suppliers within it) has a characteristic mindset that determines behaviour. Lack of shift in mindset can (over time) cause some spectacular falls from grace, such as at Marks & Spencer between 1998 and 2001, when profits halved.

## Learning point 4 – only pursue quality growth

When embarking on a path towards more growth, companies often pursue opportunities that are not easily sustainable or that will dilute shareholder returns. This needs to be counterbalanced by obsessive thinking about options, rather then pursuing the first set of growth ideas you came up with. In the 'options' phase of growth strategy, fair and balanced consideration of different routes to corporate growth – organic, acquisitive, alliance, etc. – should be made.

Growth that takes the organization too far outside the zone of what it is really capable of will also undermine the quality of growth.

## Learning point 5 – acquisitions frequently destroy shareholder value

Most acquisitions – for the reasons outlined in this book – actually dilute or destroy shareholder value. This is because the acquirer will not have as much information as the vendor (despite due diligence) because of the thrill of the chase and also because acquisitions appear to be a faster route to growth than organic routes. As a result, acquirers typically overpay for the target. Also, inexperienced acquirers are likely to destroy value during integration as they will intervene too little, too late or in the wrong areas.

### Learning point 6 – growth strategies need to be implementable

Growth strategies need to be readily implementable – and with the cunning plan. The 'how' of the strategy is just as important as the 'what' and the 'why'. Also, whilst a cunning plan is needed during the initial options stage in developing growth strategies, it is equally important during the implementation stage.

Key variables to play with here include:

- what resources mix to deploy (for example, internal versus external);

- when to implement;

- how to beat current industry practices;

- who to involve;

- how to position the growth breakthrough internally; and

- the process of implementation (for example, how will it be project managed?)

## Learning point 7 – growth strategies require obsessive attention to stakeholder management

Growth strategies require anticipating the agendas of the key stakeholders who will have some influence over the growth strategy – and over its implementation – at some stage in the process.

In many ways, the area of stakeholder management is the most difficult that needs to be tackled. Except in the most simple of organizational structures there are invariably political influences of decision making on growth strategies. This implies that stakeholder agendas need to be openly talked about and explored. The stakeholder analysis techniques in Chapter 7 have proven useful in helping managers to deal with stakeholder tensions and conflicts.

## Growth strategies for your own career

Having run through the seven key learning points of this book, let us now finally look at growth strategies for your own career.

The strategic option grid is a useful way of evaluating both new job opportunities and career changes. This can be achieved by examining a number of possible future career routes against the criteria of:

- strategic attractiveness;

- financial attractiveness;

*Smart quotes*

Growing your own career

'Well, helicopter thinking has done me good, because it has helped make lots of career moves for me. So, somewhere along the line one must see some correlation. I think helicopter thinking must have been one of the contributory factors.'

Karen Slatford, Hewlett-Packard

- implementation difficulty;

- uncertainty and risk; and

- stakeholder acceptability.

For example, if we take the case of a young chartered accountant (aged 28) contemplating different career options, these might include:

- financial controller/financial director of a strategic business unit;

- corporate treasury;

- acquisitions and mergers specialist (merchant banking); and

- management consultancy.

Figure 10.1 appraises these options. Whilst financial controller/financial director scores 'medium' on strategic (or longer-term) attractiveness and

| | Financial controller/FD 1 | Corporate treasury 2 | Acquisitions & mergers 3 | Management consultancy 4 |
|---|---|---|---|---|
| Strategic attractiveness | ✓✓ | ✓ | ✓✓✓ | ✓✓✓ |
| Financial attractiveness | ✓ | ✓✓✓ | ✓✓✓ | ✓✓ |
| Implementation difficulty | ✓✓ | ✓ | ✓✓ | ✓✓ |
| Uncertainty and risk | ✓✓✓ | ✓✓✓ | ✓ | ✓ |
| Stakeholder acceptability | ✓ | ✓✓✓ | ✓✓✓ | ✓✓✓ |

| | | | | |
|---|---|---|---|---|
| Total scores | 9 | 11 | 12 | 11 |

**Fig. 10.1**  Strategic option grid – chartered accountant.

on implementation difficulty, and 'low' on uncertainty and risk, for this particular person it is low on acceptability. This is because the thought of a more traditional, mainly reporting role is less of a turn-on (a score of 9 overall).

On the other hand, a career in corporate treasury is very attractive financially, but very difficult – counterbalanced by being of low uncertainty and highly acceptable (a score of 11 overall).

A career as an acquisitions and mergers specialist scores very highly on strategic and financial attractiveness, and on acceptability to this stakeholder, but scores as highly uncertain and of medium difficulty (a score of 12 overall).

Finally, a management consultancy career is highly attractive strategically and highly acceptable, but of medium financial attractiveness, medium difficulty and high risk (a score of 11 overall).

So, by a narrow margin, acquisitions and mergers specialist comes out the best. But hold on a minute – if this person was relatively risk-averse, subjectively this career might lag behind the corporate training and management consultancy options. Also, if we learn that this accountant is especially keen on a sixth option, 'career flexibility', then the options might score on this new criterion as follows:

- financial controller/financial director– high (3);

- corporate treasurer – low (1);

- acquisitions and mergers specialist – low (1); and

- management consultancy – high (3).

Then we get the following scores (summing up all six criteria):

- financial controller/financial director – 12;

- corporate treasurer – 13;

- acquisitions and mergers specialist – 13; and

- management consultancy – 14.

Now we have management consultancy coming out the highest, followed by corporate treasurer and acquisitions and mergers specialist (in joint second place). Financial controller/financial director has caught up considerably.

The closeness of these scores is a reflection on the subtlety of human decision-making, and not a weakness of the technique. Because of the emotional sensitivity of difficult career choices, it is imperative to use some form of quasi-objective technique like the strategic option grid to discriminate between options. The technique allows some of the trade-offs to be examined, and will help to test out underlying assumptions and values.

*Exercise – working on your own career strategy*

For a number of career options (or, more specifically, job roles) that you have in mind, ask the following questions.

- Do these rate on the strategic option grid?

- Given the relative weight which you place on these different options, how does this affect your overall view of the relative attractiveness of these options?

Other applications of the tools in this book to advancing your career include the following.

- Growth-driver and competitive-forces analysis (Chapter 2), for understanding the future prospects of all or parts of your organization.

- From-to analysis (Chapter 7), for plotting the shifts in your skills and in management style in order to develop your career to the next level.

- Value and cost drivers (Chapter 8), for understanding the potential financial attractiveness of a particular career move.

- Force-field analysis, for understanding a job's potential implementation difficulty.

- The difficulty-over-time curve, for anticipating the difficulty posed over the first six to twelve months.

- Stakeholder analysis (and stakeholder agenda analysis), for understanding the job criteria or the agendas of the interviewers, your own agendas, and the agendas of family and other close stakeholders.

- The importance–uncertainty grid, for identifying vulnerabilities – and scenarios for bringing about their dynamics.

## Suggestions for action

There are a number of areas where you can now apply the concepts and techniques of the book. These break down into:

- management meetings;

- away-days; and

- individual reflection.

Management meetings offer an excellent opportunity to apply the growth thought process. Increasingly, managers are now finding that it is permissible to use techniques like growth drivers, the strategic option grid etc., as and when needed. If this application route is taken, it is useful to position it as a way of generally getting more value out of management meetings, rather than as a one-off experiment.

Away-days offer a very natural area for applying the growth process. When separated from the cut and thrust of everyday management activity, most managers find it much easier to reflect in a strategic way. One risk, however, is that their reflections are incomplete and no actual decision is taken. Another major risk is that, whilst a decision to go ahead is taken in principle, it is not actually implemented. This can simply be due to a lack of specific ownership, a lack of project management or managers becoming overwhelmed by other priorities as they re-enter their usual roles following the away-day.

Ideally, strategic thinking about growth opportunities should occur both at regular management meetings and at away-days. Away-days should not be relied on too much to 'Save the Company's Future'.

Turning now to individual reflection, this again is a powerful way of structuring ideas on growth. The drawback here is that managers are used to thinking about their businesses by talking about them. They also do not believe that they can get as much out of strategic thinking about growth just by private reflection. Nevertheless, experience has shown that spending, say, 15 minutes of time to use one of the following tools can pay great dividends.

- Growth drivers.

- The five competitive forces.

- The strategic option grid.

- The uncertainty–influence grid.

- Stakeholder analysis.

*Smart quotes*

'Just taking a day out to do strategic thinking does make a difference, out of the day-to-day environment. Often, and this is what it is like for most people in a sales organization, you end up with weekly, quarterly, annual pressure and targets. And you get really stuck into those – the grunt and grind, and the minutiae. And you don't get a chance to step back.'

Karen Slatford, Hewlett-Packard

'It's that helicopter thing. Getting up in the helicopter and looking down. The thought that you are someone from Mars and have landed on Earth and don't have a clue – it gives you a completely fresh view. Looking-from-above – sometimes you catch yourself doing it. Sometimes I catch myself doing it in a meeting. I let them get on with it, and I go up, up. I have a look and listen. It is really good practice; you look at things from a completely different angle.'

Karen Slatford, Hewlett-Packard

*Smart quotes*

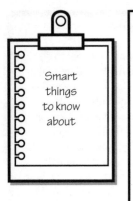

GROWTH

1  Growth is a dynamic process.
2  Growth requires imagination.
3  'Culturate' your growth mindset.
4  Only pursue quality growth.
5  Acquisitions frequently destroy shareholder value.
6  Growth strategies need to be implementable.
7  Growth strategies demand active and explicit stakeholder management.
8  The techniques can be used in management meetings, away-days or individual reflection (perhaps supported by mentoring).
9  The growth techniques can also be used to help grow your own career.

# Index

acquisitions 23, 28, 169–70, 272–3
  added value
    BMW example 172–3
    divestment 175–7
    future enhancing/protective value
      172
    future opportunity value 172
    importance–uncertainty grid scenario
      173–5
    sweat value 172
    synergistic value 172
    V1/V2/V3 approach 170–71
  alliances/joint venture projects 273–4
  case study 194–209
  deal-making 185
    acquirer's other options 186
    time-pressure to do a deal 187
    vendor's other options 186
  development 276
  formation 274–6
  good 26
  integration 187–9
    pros/cons 190–91
    success/failure 189–90
  learning checklist 192–4
  learning point 287–8
  not-so-good 26–7
  process 177–8
    success factors 178–9
  strategy 180
    detailed evaluation 184–5
    evaluating options 182–4
    understanding goals/present position
      181–2
  summary 209
AID (attractiveness/implementation-diffi-
    culty) analysis 31–2, 89–94
alien approach 101
alliances 24, 25, 28, 273–4
Alton Towers 243–7

Amazon.com 10–14
Ansoff, Igor 52

Belgo restaurant 44
*Blackadder* 15–16
BMW 28, 130–33, 172–5, 188, 240
Bowman, Cliff 147
brainstorming 98
breakthrough management *see hoshin*
business case for growth 252
    adding value 253–4
        conceivable demand 254
        contingent demand 254
        crystallized demand 254
        estimating 254–5
        key questions 255
    exit strategies 257–9
    format 252–3
    joint ventures 256–7
    key questions for compiling 259–60
    length 253
buying experience 70

call centres 138
Carroll, Lewis 15
checklists 263–4, 284
    acquisitions 272–6
    franchises 277–8
    international 278–9
    Internet 280–81
    organic growth 264–72
    organizational capability 281–3
Columbo approach 98, 99–100
competitive forces *see* five competitive
        forces
competitors
    beating 107–8
    profiling/analysis 140–43
        exercise 143–4
cost-drivers *see* value-/cost-driver analysis

creative process 98
cunning plans 14, 15–16, 92, 107,
    222–3
customer life-cycles 70
customer value 133–9

Davies, Phil 84, 103, 149, 150, 155,
    227
difficulty-over-time curves 93, 224–6
Dilbert 89
do-it-yourself (DIY) market 54–6
dot.com market 40–43
Dyson Appliances 21, 83–4, 287
    challenges
        customer learning 88
        growth potential 89
        imitation 88
        organizational resources 89
    creating 'built-in success' 85–6
    fishbone analysis 84–8
    going for competitive knockout 84–5
Dyson, James 83, 86

easyJet 39
energy industry deregulation 56
exit strategies 257–9
external drivers 73
    airline market 39
    analysis 39
    definition 39
    dot.com shares 40–43
    increased learning about products/
        services 38
    in practice 40
    price reductions 38
    service innovation 38
    technology innovation 38

facilitators
    activities 148–9

capabilities 151–2
internal 150–51
types 149–50
fishbone analysis
acquisition integration 189
benefits 80
case studies 80, 83–9
constraints 78–80
generic systems 77–8
guidelines 76–7
opportunities 81–2
when to use 81
five competitive forces 58–9
case study 59–60
analysis 64–5
buyer power 60–61
competitive rivalry 63
cross-cultural problems 65–6
entrants 62–3
substitutes 61–2
supplier power 63
customer life-cycle/buying experience 70
industry mindset addition 67–9
start-ups 71–2
summary 66–7
football industry 1589
growth options 166
industry change 165
industry context 159–60
Manchester United 160–66
value-creating activities 163–5
force-field analysis 221–4
succession issues 158
Forte *see* Granada vs Forte
fox strategy 106–7
franchises 277–8
from-to (FT) analysis 212–14
exercise 214–15
performing 214
funeral services industry 59–67, 287

Gantt chart 219–20
gap analysis 8
benefits 9
drawbacks 9
GE (General Electric) grid 124–7
benefits 127–8
case study 130–33
in practice 128–30
Go 39
Goal Theory 103
Granada vs Forte
acquisition strategy/portfolio 199–200
acquisition values 207
background 194–5
bid 200–203
first year in charge 203–6
Forte's current strategic/financial position 195–9
key lessons 206–9
Gray, John 133
growth
competitive forces 58–72
constraints 75
creating options 29
cycle 16–19, 146
diagnosing 29, 146
drivers 37–58
evaluating 30
goals 1–2
implementing 30, 147
learning points
acquisitions frequently destroyer shareholder value 287–8
culturate growth market 287
dynamic process 286
imagination requirement 286
need for obsessive attention to stakeholder management 289
only pursue quality 287
own career 289–95

strategies need to be implementable
  288
summary 296
learning/control 30–31
options 146–7
process/techniques 28–32
review/control 147
routes 23–8
strategy/plans 4–5, 14–23, 147
understanding objectives 3
Grundy, Tony 2, 145

Hamel, Gary 57, 69, 100, 104, 105, 110,
  212
Hanson plc 191
helicopter thinking 102
Hewlett-Packard (HP) 91–2
Hodgson, Howard 62–3
*hoshin* (breakthrough management) 92,
  96–9
how-how analysis 217–21
hygiene factors *see* motivator-hygiene factors

implementation 30, 147, 211–12
  advanced issue diagnosis 215–17
  difficulty-over-time curves 224–6
  force-field analysis 221–4
  integrating strategies 235
  project scoping 217–21
  scoping 212–15
  stakeholder agenda analysis
    233–4
  stakeholder analysis 226–33
industry mindset 67–70
internal drivers 43, 73
  Belgo restaurant 44
  brakes on 43
international growth 278–9
Internet 40–43, 280–81

joint ventures 256–7, 273–4

Kama Sutra approach 211–12

Leahey, Terry 8
Leclerc, Michel 65–6
lines of enquiry
  beating your competitors 107
    build barriers to imitation 108
    learn how things are done 108
    study competitors 107
  challenging constraints 102–3
    focus on one at a time 103
    get more excited 103
    why it exists 103
  challenging industry rules 108
    abandon existing mindset 109
    change rules of the game 108
    change rules now 109
    competitive advantage 110
    what would put competitors off-bal-
      ance 109
  Columbo approach 99–114
  creating
    go back to what you really, really
      want 101
    helicopter thinking 102
    imagine the future 101
    investment/value 102
    look at existing practices 101
    simplify process 102
    start from low resource-base and
      build up 102
    work backwards from result 100
    zero-base strategy 102
  creating greater degrees of freedom 110
    ask unconscious mind for solution
      113
    be your own consultant 113
    create white space 112

eliminate unnecessary turn-offs 111
explain problem 113
forget that anyone might be against
    solution 112
get more influence 111–12
have strategic amnesty 110
imagine you just started organization
    today 111
leave problem for later 113
look for problem solving process
    113–14
move from cunning to stunning 113
remember Winnie the Pooh 111
structure brainstorming 114
think out loud 112
what is the bait 111
who might think of creative idea 112
working backwards from customers
    103–4
add value to customer 105
avoid destroying/diluting value 105
be your own customer 104
capture value 106
cunning plans 107
do psychic market research 104
financial value of product/service 107
get customer to sell for you 106–7
increasing irresistible factor 106
value creation 106

Madonna 2
Mancey, Paul 7, 89
Manchester United 21, 157, 160–66, 287
Marks & Spencer 18, 287
Milne, A.A. 111, 170, 211
Mintzberg, Henry 19–20
Mission Impossible (MI) 92, 93
mission statement 82
Mitford, Jessica 60
motivator-hygiene factors 133–4

benefits 139
dis-benefits 139
exercise 138–9
graphic illustration 136–8
not-so-smart approach 134–6

octopus grid 114–16
benefits 116
organic development 24, 25, 28
organic growth 264
market projects 266–7
new distribution channels 270–71
new technologies 271–2
new value-creating activities 269
product projects 265–6
selling more to existing customers
    267–8
organizational
breakthroughs 158
capability 156–8
    case study 158–66
    information systems 282–3
    restructuring 281–2
    successful 167
speed 31–2
weaknesses 158
own career strategy 289–90
exercise 292–3
suggestions for action 294–5

parallel work activities 220
Pioneer UK 92
piranha analysis 215–17
Porter, Michael 42, 58–9
Prahalad, C.K. 57, 69, 100, 104, 105, 110,
    212
project management 221
Prudential insurance company 213–14

Ranger, Jo 97, 152

Rover Group 172–5, 188, 240

scenarios 51–3
    benefits 58
    cross-testing 57
    definition 51–3
    discontinuity 52
    lessons learnt 57–8
    in practice 53–6
    role-play 56
    succession issues 158
    transitional events 52
Service Corporation International (SCI) 63
shareholder value 287–8
Slatford, Karen 149, 223
Spice Girls' strategy 101
Spottiswode, Jane 61
stakeholder agenda analysis 233–4
    turn-ons/turn-offs 234
stakeholder analysis 226–31
    case study 231–3
    grid 230
    levels of agenda 229
start-ups 71
    customer needs 71, 72
    customer target 71
    distribution 72
    how 72
    value activities 72
Steele, Murray 70, 150
Stelios 39
strategic amnesia 80
strategic option grid 117–19
    applying 122–3
    financial attractiveness 120
    implementation difficulty 120–21
    railway telephone enquiry system 118
    stakeholder acceptability 121
    strategic attractiveness 119
    succession issues 158

uncertainty and risk 121
strategy 84, 89
    AID analysis 89–94
    cunning plans 14, 15–16
    definitions 4–5, 14
    deliberate 19, 21
    detergent 20, 22
    emergency 20, 22
    emergent 19–20, 22
    fishbone analysis 76–89
    mix 20–21, 22–3
    submergent 20, 22
    Tarzan 24
succession issues 157–8
Sun Tzu 95, 96, 107
SWOT (strengths, weaknesses, opportunities, threats) analysis 45, 67

Tarzan strategy 24
telecommunications 53–4
Tesco 5–8, 27, 78–9
Thurso, Lord 82, 225, 239

uncertainty grids
    appraisal 46–7
    assumptions 46–8
    benefits 49
    data collection 47–8
    focus 50
    importance–uncertainty 45–9
    misunderstood 48
    in practice 48–9
    prioritize 46
    select 45
    uncertainty–influence 49–50
    uncovering the Big Thing 49

value
    intangibles 240–42
        integrative case 243–6

interdependencies 238–9
summary 261
systems 166
value-/cost-driver analysis
benefits 251
definition 247
examples 247–51
Virgin Group 23–4

Welch, Jack 110
wishbone analysis
acquisition integration 190
succession issues 158
workshops 152–3
content structure 154–6
'P' behaviours 157
running 153–4